Why the Civil War?

Why the Civil War?

★

Otto Eisenschiml

The Bobbs - Merrill Company, Inc.

Indianapolis ★ New York

Acknowledgments

IN THE WRITING of this book I have been given help by many people and organizations, to all of whom I wish to express my hearty appreciation—

To Paul M. Angle, Robert S. Henry, David C. Mearns, E. B. Long, Ralph Newman, Wayne C. Temple and the late Benjamin P. Thomas for valuable assistance.

To Joseph L. Eisendrath, Jr., for making available to me his library and collections, for reading the manuscript, for making appropriate suggestions, and for checking my references.

To Margaret Scriven of the Chicago Historical Society for her generous and cheerful co-operation.

To Marion Blashek for doing some excellent research work.

To Veronica Carroll, Marion F. Holtz, Christina Sarantakis and Gertrud Wadenpohl for help in preparing the manuscript and for transcribing my penciled notes into readable form.

To the following individuals and organizations for permission to use their copyrighted material:

Miss Esther Aldrich, Calais, Vermont (Ida M. Tarbell, *The Life of Abraham Lincoln*).

The American Historical Association, Washington, D. C. (*The Diary of Edward Bates*).

Appleton-Century-Crofts, Inc., New York (Mary Boykin Chesnut, *A Diary from Dixie*).

Dodd, Mead & Company, Inc., New York (James G. Randall, *Lincoln the President*).

Doubleday & Company, Inc., New York (*The Reminiscences of Carl Schurz;* David C. Mearns, *The Lincoln Papers*).

Harcourt, Brace and Company, Inc., New York (Carl Sandburg, *Abraham Lincoln: The War Years*).

The Historical Society of Pennsylvania, Philadelphia (Letter from Chase to Root).

Houghton Mifflin Company, Boston (*The Diary of Gideon Welles*).

The Illinois State Historical Society, Springfield (*The Diary of Orville Hickman Browning*).

The Journal of Southern History, Baton Rouge, Louisiana (Volume XVI, Ramsdell, "Lincoln and Fort Sumter.").

Alfred A. Knopf, Inc., New York (Benjamin P. Thomas, *Abraham Lincoln*).

Louisiana State University Press, Baton Rouge (Kenneth M. Stampp, *And the War Came*).

Rutgers University Press, New Brunswick, New Jersey (Roy P. Basler, ed., *The Collected Works of Abraham Lincoln*).

Charles Scribner's Sons, New York (*Dictionary of American Biography*).

The University of Illinois Press, Urbana (James G. Randall, *Constitutional Problems Under Lincoln;* Harlan Hoyt Horner, *Lincoln and Greeley*).

University of North Carolina Press, Chapel Hill (John Shipley Tilley, *Lincoln Takes Command*).

Yale University Press, New Haven (David M. Potter, *Lincoln and His Party in the Secession Crisis*).

Contents

★

Why the Civil War?

Foreword

THIS BOOK does not concern itself with the campaigns and battles of the Civil War. It deals rather with intriguing questions which seem to call for answers.

Was the conflict really irrepressible? If not, who started it? Did Lincoln, acting secretly because of political considerations, sincerely try to avert war? Did a heavy storm at sea, an unendorsed order and the disobedience of a Confederate officer frustrate his plan for preserving peace?

Did the bloodless bombardment of Fort Sumter necessarily precipitate civil war? What was the true meaning of Lincoln's proclamation calling for 75,000 troops? And why did he announce the "probable" purpose for which they were to be employed?

As I delved into these and other questions, new ones constantly arose. In addition, many apparent incongruities presented themselves, for which I have sought explanations. I offer here the results of my re-examination, in an endeavor to shed more light on some aspects of the Civil War which are still shrouded in obscurity.

Civil War Did Not

Seem Necessary

WHEN LINCOLN TOOK OVER the duties of chief executive he was steeped in the ways of domestic politics
but lacked experience in broader fields. No other
"experiment so rash had ever been made," wrote
Charles Francis Adams, Lincoln's minister to Great
Britain, "as that of elevating to the head of affairs a
man with so little previous preparation for his task."[1]
Gideon Welles, Lincoln's Secretary of the Navy, did
not think this statement grossly exaggerated.[2] Lord
Lyons, the British minister in Washington, thought
that while Lincoln apparently knew backwoods village
politics, he had yet to demonstrate his ability to command respect in the national arena.[3] But though most
people felt that Lincoln was out of his depth at the be-

13

ginning, even the skeptics admitted he was growing
rapidly. Unfortunately, the weeks allowed him for
growth were short, the problems calling for immediate decisions desperately urgent. Would he be
able to compose the differences between the two sections of the country? Or was civil war unavoidable?

Lincoln shared the conviction held by most Ameri-
cans in both North and South that, except for slavery,
every issue separating them could be settled peaceably. Looking back at four years of strife, he was to
put it succinctly in his Second Inaugural. "These
slaves," he said, "constituted a peculiar and powerful
interest. All knew that this interest was, somehow, the
cause of the war."⁴

In 1861, however, slavery was already on the way
out. As long as manufacturing was done on the plan-
tation and there were cheap raw materials at hand,
slaves yielded a profit, despite the fact that for each
working slave a number of nonproductive dependents
had to be fed, housed, clothed and provided with
medical care. But machines had begun to displace
human muscles, and when factory-made goods could
be bought for less money than those produced by slave
labor, bondsmen began changing from an economic
asset to a financial liability. In the border states the
number of slaves in proportion to freemen had been
declining for several years, and the trend was beginning to spread through the Deep South. Quietly but
steadily slavery, and with it the sole explosive factor
in the political situation, was passing out of existence.⁵
If an armed conflict could be warded off for another

generation, all controversial issues would resolve themselves without bloodletting. The fate of the nation depended on whether Lincoln would act in line with this prospect.

In days past, whenever the sectional disputes had threatened to get out of control, statesmen on both sides buried their party differences while they patched up matters. In 1850 Clay, Webster and Douglas had worked out a series of compromises with which they expected to hold the Union together. Clay told Jefferson Davis that he thought peace had been made secure for thirty years,[6] after which it was believed that slavery would have become extinct through natural causes. As events proved, he had set his hopes too high. The dam that was to outlast slavery was being eroded by hotheaded, notoriety-hungry politicians, of whom both the North and South had a generous share, who did their utmost to inflame the population. Luckily, their efforts met with indifferent success. The common men continued to do their daily chores in silence, wanting only peace, as common men have done since the beginning of time. The mouthings of rabble-rousers and the forecasts of war to come sounded hollow to them. America was a democracy. People figured on being given a chance to vote on vital issues before being engulfed in a life-and-death struggle.

In November 1860 Lincoln was elected, and in the following month South Carolina seceded. The Southern end of the dam had given way. Senator Crittenden then offered a compromise which was fervently supported by public-spirited citizens throughout the country. Said Senator Pugh:

The . . . proposition has been indorsed by the almost unanimous vote of the Legislature of Kentucky. . . . It has been petitioned for by a larger number of electors of the United States than any proposition that was ever before Congress. I believe in my heart today, that it would carry an overwhelming majority of . . . nearly every State in the Union.[7]

Despite its popular endorsement the bill failed to pass; but the Peace Convention, which met in Washington a few weeks later, inspired new hope. Acting as presiding officer, former President Tyler exclaimed in his opening address that the eyes of the whole nation were turned to the assembly. If it could preserve peace, one long, loud shout of joy would resound throughout the land.[8] That he spoke truly was attested by a response so rousing that it had few precedents, if any. Participants in mass meetings everywhere demanded a conciliatory attitude. Petitions carrying thousands of signatures swamped the delegates. Leading newspapers counseled moderation. To the average citizen civil war was inconceivable.

During his journey to Washington Lincoln himself diagnosed the situation accurately: "There is no crisis but an artificial one . . . gotten up . . . by designing politicians. My advice . . . is to keep cool." If both factions controlled their tempers, there would be an end to the agitation.[9]

When Lincoln entered the White House, conditions still favored a return to tranquillity. The Confederacy had been formed in February; anticipated and discounted, the event had created little excitement. In many quarters it was greeted with a sigh of relief. Gideon Welles observed that "secession was considered by most persons as a political party question, not as rebellion."[10]

During the month preceding Inauguration Day, nothing startling had happened. The border states had stayed in the Union. Tennessee and North Carolina had voted against secession. Arkansas and Missouri had remained neutral. Kentucky had taken no action. Virginia had elected a state convention in which the Union element predominated. The cotton states had gained their independence, and the Northern abolitionists had been glad to see them go. The troublemakers had little left to shout about; nothing appeared in sight to refoment the diminishing discord.

One cloud still cast a shadow over the land, and that was Fort Sumter. Yet this southern outpost was of no greater importance than many others, including a long string of arsenals, mints, customhouses and navy yards, that had fallen to the Secessionists. The North had taken these losses in its stride. Had Sumter been evacuated, there might have been some grumbling, but no demand for war. Douglas, whose patriotism was above reproach, gave voice to a widely shared view by contending that inasmuch as the Confederates were the *de facto* government of South Carolina the fort should be turned over to them.[11]

Attorney General Edward Bates, in a written opinion, made a statesmanlike summary of the case.

This is not a question of lawful right . . . but of prudence. . . . The wisdom of the act must be tested by the value of the object to be gained. . . . It may indeed involve a point of honor or a point of pride, but I do not see any great national interest involved. . . . I am willing to evacuate fort Sumter.[12]

Lincoln had expressed a similar idea in his Inaugural when he referred to the filling of Southern Federal offices from which the appointees had resigned. "While the strict legal right may exist in the government," he said, "to enforce the exercise of these offices, the attempt . . . would be so irritating . . . that I deem it better to forego, for the time, the uses of such offices."[13]   This was not entirely correct, for it was not the President's right but his sworn duty to fill the Federal offices. Nevertheless he would not "force obnoxious strangers" on local populations. The garrison of the South Carolina fort surely was more obnoxious to the Secessionists than civilian officeholders would have been. Furthermore, Lincoln had promised in his speech that he would execute the laws only insofar as practicable. The peace-loving populace heartily applauded these dispassionate statements.

Fort Sumter, however, was not the only potential trouble spot on the map. Close to the Gulf shore of Florida, on an island at the entrance to Pensacola Bay, stood Fort Pickens, in which a small Union garrison was confronted by vastly superior Southern forces.

Nevertheless, neither of the two places offered an immediate threat to peace. At Pensacola a truce had been agreed on and was being kept in good faith by all concerned. Charleston Harbor also was quiescent, the authorities remaining on a friendly footing with the commanding officer of Fort Sumter, Major Robert Anderson. They knew that he was short of provisions and would soon have to surrender.

All that was needed for a happy ending to an unhappy situation was to do nothing. Buchanan had shown the way, and Lincoln seemed inclined to follow in his footsteps. After a meeting with Vice President Hamlin shortly after the election, Lincoln let it be known that a "programme of 'masterly inactivity'" would be "strictly carried out."[14] It was a wise decision, for rarely in history has a vexing problem presented such an easy solution. If the two rival governments exercised patience, time would do the rest. "Civil War . . . did not at the moment seem imminent or necessary," wrote Nicolay and Hay. "Lincoln had declared . . . that he would not begin it; Jefferson Davis had written . . . to the commissioners that he did not desire it."[15]

On the day of Lincoln's inauguration the political barometer pointed to clearing skies and fair weather.

2

Lincoln Maneuvers

For Peace

THE NEW PRESIDENT was facing two problems of prime importance. That of the two forts was incidental but required immediate attention; the second, which concerned slavery, was fundamental and called for a long-range program. If Lincoln could dispose of both problems, he would eliminate the danger of war.

Lincoln's views on slavery were well known. He had repeatedly stated that he abhorred it on moral grounds and opposed its extension, but that he was powerless and unwilling to interfere with it where it existed. He believed that a change should and would be accomplished through the ballot box, not through what contemporary writers were wont to call "the arbitrament of the sword." His only public utterance which could possibly be construed as warlike was his "house divided" speech, in which he had said that

20

eventually America would have to be either all slave
or all free. He held this remark, made in 1858, to be a
prediction, not a threat. To read a meaning into it
which had not been intended, he scorned as political
trickery.

"There need be no war" had been the leitmotiv of
Lincoln's uniformly peaceful speeches on his way to
Washington. He did stress, however, that nothing
could ever bring him to "consent to the destruction of
the Union," and that there must be no further appeasement. He made this very clear in an address at Tren-
ton, where he said that no man was more devoted to
peace than he was, but that he wanted the people to
support him, should it become necessary to "put the
foot down firmly."[1] The next day he dulled the sharp
edge of these words by declaring that "there is no
need of bloodshed . . . unless it be forced upon the
Government."[2] In a somewhat different form he repeated this in his First Inaugural, saying there could
be no conflict unless his "dissatisfied fellow country-
men" chose to be the aggressors.[3]

In his private utterances Lincoln was considerably
less pacific. With his nomination still in doubt, he had
sent a message to his campaign manager, David Davis,
in which he endorsed Seward's idea of an "irrepressible conflict."[4] Shortly after South Carolina had
seceded, and threatened to take possession of the forts
in Charleston Harbor, Lincoln asked General Winfield
Scott confidentially to be prepared "to either *hold*, or
retake, the forts, as the case may require, at, and after
the inauguration."[5] At the same time he wrote to New
York Congressman P. H. Silvester that if the [Charles-

ton] forts were surrendered, they must be retaken.[6]
On December 24, 1860, he expressed himself forcibly
in a letter to Senator Lyman Trumbull: ". . . if our
friends at Washington concur, announce publicly at
once that they [the forts at Charleston] are to be
retaken after the inauguration."[7] Retaking the forts
meant war. To Alexander H. Stephens, who was to
be elected Vice President of the Confederacy a few
weeks later, he was still more outspoken. He declared
it to be his resolve that North and South should remain
one country even if the bond of brotherhood had to
be riveted by force.[8] That Lincoln was pessimistic
as to the preservation of peace is indicated by almost
identical letters he sent to Senators Lyman Trumbull
and William Kellogg in the beginning of December
1860, when a compromise on the extension of slavery
was under discussion. "The tug has to come, & better
now than any time hereafter,"[9] he wrote. These were
not hopeful omens.

When Lincoln assumed the Presidency, his avowed
credo still was no war, but no more appeasement. In
his inaugural address he offered the South an olive
branch, but the outline of a sword was visible beneath
its leaves. The offer was not unlike that of the Roman
emissary to Carthage who declared that he held peace
in one hand, war in the other, and that the Carthagin-
ians could choose between them. The choice between
the sword and the olive branch, Lincoln implied, lay
with the Secessionists.

Despite these warlike utterances Lincoln was nurs-
ing a secret plan by which he hoped to preserve peace.
This plan, which probably had sprung from the nimble

mind of Secretary of State William Seward, was a compromise between sternness and moderation. It contemplated reinforcement of Fort Pickens, but withdrawal from Fort Sumter. This would eliminate the most pressing difficulty, for few people cared or even knew a great deal about Fort Pickens, while Fort Sumter had been in the limelight since December 26, 1860, when Major Robert Anderson had occupied it on his own initiative. Situated in plain view of Charleston, the birthplace of secession, the fort was an irritant and a threat to the local population, a combustible which might burst into flame on the slightest provocation. Lincoln's plan was simple enough, but it would take clever maneuvering to bring it to fruition.

Up to March 11 the President took no overt action pertaining to the seceded states. From then on happenings began to crowd one another in quick succession. Some seemed of little moment at the time, but became of consequence later; others had an immediate and decisive impact on the relations between the two sections of the country. Woven together into one piece, each event played its part in forming the groundwork for grave events which were in the immediate offing.

The developments regarding Fort Pickens followed one another at irregular intervals:

March 12, 1861. The warship *Mohawk* is dispatched to the Pensacola harbor with orders issued "by command of General Scott" to reinforce Fort Pickens and hold it. The *Mohawk* is expected to arrive in about eleven days.

March 28, 1861. Having received no news of the

reinforcement, the President spends a sleepless night, and on

March 29, 1861, prepares a second expedition to Pensacola.

March 31, 1861. The *Mohawk* arrives at Pensacola, but the senior navy officer refuses to obey Scott's order.

April 6, 1861. Lincoln is officially notified that the order has not been carried out, and sends a navy officer by rail to Pensacola with instructions to have the order obeyed.

April 6, 1861. The second expedition sails from New York with instructions to reinforce Fort Pickens even at the risk of opening hostilities; but on

April 12-13, 1861, prior to its arrival, the fort is reinforced peaceably.

April 13-14, 1861. News of the peaceful reinforcement is published in Washington.

The developments relating to Fort Sumter were of a more complex character:

March 12 to April 7, 1861. Secretary Seward repeatedly intimates to Confederate Commissioners in Washington that Fort Sumter will be evacuated.

March 15, 1861. A majority of Lincoln's Cabinet votes to abandon the work.

March 21, 1861. Gustavus V. Fox, a former navy officer, arrives at Sumter to gather on-the-spot information.

March 25, 1861. Ward H. Lamon, Lincoln's former law partner, visits Charleston and leaves the impression with Major Anderson, Governor Francis Pickens of South Carolina and Commanding General Pierre G. T. Beauregard that Fort Sumter is about to be given up.

March 29, 1861. The Cabinet, polled once more, is divided between reinforcing and vacating Fort Sumter.

At this juncture the lack of news from Pensacola causes a sudden change in Lincoln's plan.

March 29, 1861. The President personally issues directions to prepare an expedition "to be in readiness for sea service." That Charleston is its destination is not announced.

April 1, 1861. The Confederate government orders General Beauregard to stop supplying the garrison with provisions of any kind, but Beauregard does not comply at once.

April 4, 1861. Lincoln confers with several Northern governors.

April 4, 1861. John B. Baldwin, a Unionist member of the Virginia Convention, confers with Lincoln. He is informed that a few days before, the President had been ready to withdraw from Fort Sumter in exchange for adjournment *sine die* of the Virginia Convention, but, Baldwin is told, "now it is too late."

Because of a disturbing letter from Anderson, another change in the program now becomes necessary.

April 4, 1861. Lincoln advises Anderson that an expedition is being prepared to relieve him, but that he may capitulate at his discretion.

April 4, 1861. Fox is put in charge of the expedition.

April 5, 1861. The vessels comprising this expedition are ordered to rendezvous off Charleston on April 11.

April 8, 1861. A messenger from Lincoln informs the governor of South Carolina that Fort Sumter will be supplied with provisions only, that if this is not resisted, no effort will be made to throw in men, arms and ammunitions without further notice.

April 8 to 10, 1861. The ships of the Sumter expedition depart.

April 11, 1861. The Confederate government, advised that part of the relief fleet has been sighted near the entrance of Charleston harbor, demands immediate surrender of Fort Sumter.

April 12, 1861. Following Anderson's unsatisfactory reply, bombardment begins.

April 12-13, 1861. The Federal fleet arrives off Charleston harbor but takes no part in the fighting despite orders to the contrary. Shortly afterward its commander is promoted.

April 14, 1861. Fort Sumter surrenders. No casualties from enemy fire are reported by either side.

April 15, 1861. Lincoln issues a call for 75,000 militia on his sole responsibility.

At first glance it would appear that these events, in conjunction with all others since the day of Lincoln's nomination, followed a consistent pattern; yet on close examination curious inconsistencies are easily discovered. Why did Lincoln, after endorsing Seward's "irrepressible conflict" idea in May, announce a do-nothing policy in November, then confidentially advise

Scott a few weeks later that the Charleston forts must be retaken? And if the Charleston forts, why not other lost Federal property? Why did the President urge peace on his way to Washington, yet privately express warlike thoughts?

Who was guilty of sending an important order to Pensacola in such a form that it was not, in fact could not be, obeyed? Why did Lincoln send additional reinforcements there before he knew that his original order had not been carried out?

Why did Federal warships stand idly by while Fort Sumter was under fire, although Fox, the commander of the expedition, had instructions to force his way into the harbor? And why was Fox, despite his insubordination, promoted to a high position shortly afterward?

Why did Lincoln declare that April 4 was too late for the evacuation of Sumter, after considering such a move feasible a few days before? And how could he offer to trade off a Federal fort without violating his doctrine of an indivisible country? Finally, and surpassing all other questions in importance: did war between people, who had so long lived peaceably as one nation, inescapably follow the bloodless bombardment of a militarily useless fort?

These questions, challenging though they are, have received little attention from modern writers; yet they were not entirely overlooked by contemporary commentators.

A New York author named Robert Tomes, in a work published in 1862 and titled *The War with the*

South,[10] was concerned about the inactivity of the warships during the Sumter bombardment:

The want of concert of action between Major Anderson and the fleet has been a source of perplexity.
Some have attributed it to the fact that the message
to him, conveying the intention of his Government, had
been studiously withheld by the authorities at Charleston. Others, however, have surmised that it was never
seriously designed to expose the armed vessels to the
fire of the Charleston forts, and that Major Anderson,
made aware of this circumstance through his private
dispatches, had acted accordingly.

Then Tomes presented a third possibility:

It has also been suggested that the administration at
Washington had intended only to make a demonstra-
tion of force, without contemplating the exercise
of it. . . .

A New England journalist was less troubled by the
mysterious happenings of the early war days than he
was about the propriety of making public what he
knew. J. G. Holland, a member of the Massachusetts
Historical Society and the author of an early Lincoln
biography, had been chief editor of the *Springfield*
(Massachusetts) *Republican* during 1862, in which
capacity he probably had gained considerable inside
information. "Many of the revelations . . . of the first
few weeks [of Lincoln's incumbency]," he wrote
temptingly in November 1865, "would doubtless be
startling, even today, but the time has not come for

their exposure." This was a peculiar statement for a historical writer to make. What were his grounds for hinting at some important information which had been suppressed? What would the "startling revelations" have disclosed? And if "even today" was too early for their exposure after the lapse of four and a half years, what future time did Holland consider safe?[11] Ten years? Fifty? A hundred? With Lincoln gone, whom was he trying to protect? Was it the reputation of some person or persons still living, or was it the memory of the dead President?

Holland lived until 1881, but though he remained a prolific writer for the remainder of his life he never again returned to the Lincoln theme. It is a matter of regret that a man of his talents and opportunities, who stood so close to the scene, chose to rob future historians of interesting material which now may be forever lost.

So far as is known, no other writer, contemporary or otherwise, has exercised his birthright of historical curiosity by turning the spotlight on this jumbled mass of confusing evidence, and it has been accepted without the searching analysis which clearly seems to have been called for.

The detailed story of the events which transpired between March 12 and April 15, 1861, illuminates the difficulties of the problems with which the President had to contend during that period; but what he wished to accomplish by his skillful maneuvering denoted statesmanship of a high order. Holding Fort Pickens and letting Fort Sumter go would save face all around.

If an armed conflict could be prevented at all, this compromise would avert it. Before abandoning Fort Sumter, however, possession of the feebly held Fort Pickens had to be made secure. To give up the Charleston stronghold without an assertion of authority at some other point would be interpreted as a sign of weakness and have dangerous repercussions. Absolute secrecy of the plan was, of course, a *sine qua non* to its success.

Time was precious, and on March 11 the President set the wheels in motion. At his direction General Scott issued an order to Captain I. Vogdes, commander of the troops at Pensacola, to throw additional men into Fort Pickens,[12] regardless of a truce which had been agreed on under President Buchanan, but which Lincoln did not consider binding on the new administration. If carried out stealthily, there was little risk that this coup would be resisted; and the President further minimized the danger by taking only the leading participants into his confidence, so as not to alert the Confederate government or stir up dissension at home. Even the members of his Cabinet, with the exception of Seward, were left in ignorance. Seward felt sure of success, and hinted to the Southern Commissioners that the evacuation of Sumter would be consummated within ten days. Then Fate capriciously took a hand in the game and ruined it completely.

To keep the message to Captain Vogdes from falling into Secessionist hands, it was dispatched by the warship *Mohawk,* which was expected to reach Pensacola on or about the twenty-third of March. The reinforcement of Fort Pickens should have been effected a day or two later, but the vessel was delayed and did not arrive until the thirty-first. This annoying upset could have been endured, had the arrival been followed by prompt action. Unfortunately, this was not the case. Captain Vogdes requisitioned the necessary landing boats from Captain H. A. Adams, commander of the Gulf fleet. Adams, however, claimed he was constrained by a previous order, signed by Secretary of War Holt and Secretary of the Navy Toucey of Buchanan's Cabinet, and refused to obey instructions, signed by a general, which ran counter to those he held from higher quarters. Complying with Scott's directive would be "in direct violation of the orders from the Navy Department under which I am acting," he wrote.[13] If the order had come from the Secretary of the Navy, or had borne Lincoln's endorsement, Adams would have obeyed it. To make matters worse, because of lack of communications his noncompliance did not immediately become known in Washington, leaving Lincoln in a turmoil of doubt and uncertainty.

Failure to attach his signature or have the order issued through the Navy Department may be accounted for by the President's inexperience in military routine, but Scott's negligence cannot be dismissed so lightly. Scott had frequently given indications that he felt called upon to determine the policy of the government. He had gone on record to say that neither Fort Pickens nor Fort Sumter could be held with the means at hand, and had recommended that both be given up.[14] Was he conspiring against his Chief in the honest conviction that he was acting in the best interest of the country? But whatever prompted his delinquency, it was one

of the many apparently insignificant incidents which
changed history.

The haste with which the expedition to Fort Pickens
had been organized proved another stumbling block.
Since no preparations for unforeseen exigencies had
been made, the President remained uninformed of the
impasse which had developed. Elementary prudence
should have dictated that a trustworthy agent be sta-
tioned at the Gulf to relay plain or coded messages
between Washington and the navy commander. The
Confederates at Pensacola were lenient. They let
Union officers visit Captain Adams as late as April 12,
much to their subsequent regret. Up to that day even
newspaper correspondents at Pensacola were allowed
to send wires to their Northern employers. A telegraphic order to a local government representative
would have caused Fort Pickens to be reinforced upon
the arrival of the *Mohawk*, in which case Lincoln
could have yielded Fort Sumter before the growing
tension aggravated the difficulties of the problem.

The importance of a well-designed communication
system between Washington and the Southern forts
should have been evident. It had occurred to Captain
(later General) Abner Doubleday, then serving at
Fort Sumter, long before a crisis was reached. Fear-
ing that sooner or later the correspondence with his
brother in New York would be tampered with, he
invented a cipher, through which he sent valuable intelligence to Lincoln at Springfield and to other leading Northerners.[15] The President might have profited
by this example and taken steps to keep in touch with

his distant commanders, if he had had more time to familiarize himself with the national scene and if he had not tried to do too many things at once. His secretaries recalled sympathetically:

All this was done, . . . not in the retirement which gives calm reflection, but . . . in the confusion of conflicting counsel, . . . the . . . atmosphere of treason and insurrection, . . . and the daily defection of Government officials.[16]

While this explains Lincoln's neglect of taking such a simple precaution, it does not excuse it. Despite Nicolay's and Hay's doubts, Washington did not lack in men as trustworthy as themselves. If the President had appointed a capable assistant to work out the particulars of the Pickens and Sumter affairs, he would have gone far toward insuring the success of his program.

While the *Mohawk* was plowing laboriously toward her destination, another matter had to be looked into. Before evacuating Fort Sumter, Lincoln had to get reliable data on two points: how long could the work hold out, and was provisioning feasible, either peaceably or by force? In other words, how strong was his bargaining position in negotiating a withdrawal?

In pursuance of this thought he sent G. V. Fox, a relative of Postmaster General Blair, to Charleston for first-hand information.[17] Fox, who was a former navy officer, had urged reinforcement of Fort Sumter as

early as January. He had proposed sending troops and
provisions on a large steamer, then transferring them
to the island fortress on tugboats. A warship was to
act as escort and as a base of supplies.[18] He would
now see if this stratagem was still workable; but the
main purpose of his trip was to furnish the President
facts on which to base further action.

Fox met Anderson on March 21. He was told that
even if the garrison were at once put on short rations
the food would not last beyond noon of April 15, unless
further supplies were received.[19] By this Anderson
meant supplies from his own government, for the mar-
kets of Charleston were open to him, although in a
limited way. He added, however, that he would not
reduce the food allowances, unless he received orders
to that effect from Washington. To attempt landing
provisions by force he considered suicidal. He expressed this view so emphatically that Fox did not
mention the possibility of a relief plan to him.[20]

On March 25 Ward Lamon, Lincoln's friend and
erstwhile law partner, arrived in Charleston and held
conversations with Governor Pickens, General Beauregard and Major Anderson. All three received the
impression that the garrison would leave within a few
days.[21] Anderson ordered work on the fortifications
stopped, began to take inventory, made arrangements
to procure transports for his men and had his books,
drawings and hospital supplies packed up.[22] "The remarks made to me by Colonel Lamon," he wrote to
the War Department on April 4, ". . . have induced
me . . . to believe that orders would soon be issued

for my abandoning this work."[23] There is no doubt
that at the time of his visit Lamon truly reflected Lincoln's intention; so did Seward. Lincoln's Secretary of
State was not adverse to political double talk at times,
but in his dealings with the Confederate Commissioners he was unquestionably sincere, all claims by Southern sympathizers notwithstanding.

The reason for Lamon's visit has never been made
clear. Several writers have suggested that Lincoln
wished him to appraise Southern sentiment, but this
explanation lacks plausibility. Fox had left Charleston
on the evening of the twenty-first, only four days
before Lamon's arrival, and by that time he must have
already submitted a report to the President. Furthermore, the Charleston sentiment was less important
than that of Montgomery, and both had been vocifer-
ously expressed in Southern newspapers. It is more
likely that the sole purpose of Lamon's presence in
Charleston was to advise the authorities of Anderson's
early departure. The timing of his visit supports this
assumption. Scott's order for the reinforcement of
Fort Pickens was due in Pensacola about the twenty-
third, the news of the coup could be expected to reach
Charleston on or about the twenty-fifth, and Lamon
was there to assure the Confederates that they would
be compensated for the loss of the Southern post by
the abandonment of Fort Sumter.

During Lamon's conversations with the authorities
at Charleston, he was informed that his suggestion to
have Anderson's men taken off by a war vessel was
unacceptable, because no ship of this type would be

allowed to enter the harbor unmolested under any circumstances.²⁴

When the sun set on March 28, several days had passed since the expected arrival of the *Mohawk* at Pensacola, and still no hint of anything unusual had been reported by the press which, due to the poor over-all planning, had become Washington's only source of up-to-date information. Lincoln was worried. Next morning he told his secretaries that he had not slept a wink.²⁵ He gave them no reason for his restlessness, but it may be safely surmised that he feared something had gone wrong at the Gulf. If so, the very keystone of his peace policy was gravely imperiled.

March 29 was a turning point in history, although few people recognized it as such. A Cabinet meeting was held; though it took a prominent place in the day's record, it really was quite unimportant. The members were asked again for their stand on Fort Sumter. This time their vote was about equally divided, but Lincoln paid little attention to it. While he tossed through a sleepless night his thinking had undergone a basic change. The uncertainty regarding Fort Pickens had aroused his apprehension that he might lose control of the situation, unless he put a new plan into effect. This plan, which he had worked out with great care, called for a show of strength at Fort Sumter. With this in mind, he already had prepared a confidential order, on which, with the exception of Seward, his Cabinet had not been consulted.²⁶

As soon as they stopped debating, he sent it to his Secretary of War.[27]

I desire that an expedition, to move by sea, be got ready to sail as early as the 6th of April next, the whole according to memorandum attached, and that you co-öperate with the Secretary of the Navy for that object.

A. Lincoln[28]

Attached were instructions to the Navy Department indicating the names of the ships and the number of troops desired. The purpose of the expedition was not stated. Had the Cabinet members known that it was readied for the avowed purpose of relieving Fort Sumter, they might have wondered why Lincoln had taken the trouble to ask for their opinions.

Another important item was on the day's list, but it does not appear in the records. Lincoln, by this time half-convinced that his order to reinforce Fort Pickens had not been executed, and perhaps suspecting where the responsibility lay, asked Scott for an explanation. Although the President later claimed that he had been given no clear understanding of the truce at Pensacola, he must have known of its existence, because Scott referred to it in his reply of March 30, adding that he had not learned of the restraining order to Captain Adams until a few days before, but had entertained the opinion that the truce had terminated with the Washington Peace Convention.[29] Be that as it may—and at best it would show unpardonable lassitude on his part—he did know that a navy officer need not take orders from an army general. Scott's refer-

ence to the Peace Conference manifestly was only a
convenient screen behind which he tried to hide his
mortification at having been found out.

More moves were being hatched, about which the
Cabinet was kept in the dark. That same evening a
captain of the Engineers' Corps named Montgomery
C. Meigs, whom Seward had recommended, was secretly summoned to the White House. In a conference
at which Lincoln and Seward were the only other men
present, the situation at Pickens was thoroughly can-
vassed, again under the supposition, which was rapidly becoming a certainty, that the fort had not been
reinforced. The young captain suggested that an ener-
getic officer be sent there at the head of a new expedition. He suggested Lieutenant D. D. Porter of the
Navy, an intimate friend of his, as the man best fitted
for this task. Meigs described him as a daredevil in
uniform, who once had entered the harbor of Havana
in open defiance of an order by the governor of the
island,[30] and who could be counted on to duplicate
this feat in the harbor of Pensacola.

After two days of deliberation Porter received his
instructions. He could pick any available warship to
serve as his convoy; the troops, sailing in an unarmed
transport, were to be commanded by one Colonel
Harvey Brown, whose orders had been drawn up by
Lincoln himself. Their intent could not be miscon-
strued.

You have been designated to take command of an
expedition to reenforce and hold Fort Pickens. . . .
You will proceed with the least possible delay. . . .

The naval officers in the Gulf will be instructed to cooperate with you. . . . Should a shot be fired at you, you will defend yourself . . . at whatever hazard, and, if needful for such defense, inflict upon the assailants all the damage in your power. . . .[31]

Strange words these, from the pen of a man who only a few weeks before had said to the people of the seceded states, "We are not enemies but friends. We must not be enemies." But Fort Pickens had to remain in Federal hands "at whatever hazard" or, if necessary, be repossessed. Lincoln already had written off Sumter, and he could not afford to give up both places without suffering a dangerous lowering of respect abroad and a corresponding loss of support at home.

In writing out the order to Colonel Brown, the President had made sure that this time the Navy would co-operate with the Army,[32] and that Scott would be given no opportunities for meddling. So as to close all loopholes, Seward delivered the message in person. The old general surrendered gracefully. "When the king commands," he said, "nothing is impossible."[33] He understood that Lincoln meant business and would stand for no more subterfuges. Nevertheless, on the following day, March 31, he raised fresh objections; the difficulties, he feared, were too great. Thereupon he was told point-blank that the President "wished this thing done," and that there must be no failure. The well-deserved rebuke put an end to Scott's patronizing attitude. Like Seward, he was finding out who was making the major decisions in the new regime.

Had the order to Colonel Brown been generally

known, it would have created an uproar. On March 11
Lincoln had ordered that the troops effect the strengthening of Fort Pickens "at the first favorable moment,"[34]
which indicated a desire to avoid bloodshed. Not a
word had then been said about inflicting "all possible
damage," should the Confederates interfere. Yet the
second order, despite its tone of belligerence, had
peace as its ultimate object, because in no other way
could Fort Sumter be honorably given up. As to the
possibility of inaugurating war, Lincoln was taking a
reasonable chance. Seward had given the Confederates no assurances regarding Fort Pickens; if they
made its reinforcement a *casus belli,* they would have
to bear the responsibility. Lincoln did not think they
would regard the step in this light, and subsequent
developments showed that he had adjudged the
chances correctly.

With the prospect of a secure Fort Pickens in mind,
the question of how to abandon Fort Sumter without
loss of prestige had to be considered next. Militarily,
the problem was an extremely delicate one, for Major
Anderson might well prefer death to surrender. Politically, the prospect was equally dismal. The Northern
people on the whole were apathetic and would rebel
against sacrificing men and ships to sustain a position
of no practical value. Nevertheless, the President also
had to pay heed to a small but influential minority
who clamored for vigorous action. He would be severely criticized if he tried to please either faction at
the expense of the other. In the parlance of the street,
he was damned if he did and damned if he didn't.

The way in which Lincoln endeavored to extricate

himself from this dilemma deserves the admiration even of his bitterest detractors; for no project involving such high stakes ever was designed with greater sagacity, or for a more laudable purpose. It was probably during his sleepless night that he had conceived the idea of bringing about the evacuation of Fort Sumter in a way agreeable to both Northern factions. He would placate the war party by sending an armed expedition to Fort Sumter, but he would see to it that it did no fighting. He would cater to the peace advocates by announcing that the expedition's sole purpose was to carry provisions, while making sure these were not delivered. To appease the two feuding factions was not enough, however; it was also imperative to govern the actions of the Confederates and those of Major Anderson, and Lincoln had given due attention to both. In order to hold the Confederates in check, the definite abandonment of Fort Sumter would be made known to them in advance, thus removing the necessity of their using force. As to Anderson, he would be made to yield through lack of food, thereby insuring an honorable surrender.

This fourfold plan, though startlingly bold in conception and bristling with difficulties, was nonetheless feasible, provided it was thoroughly prepared and carefully timed. Proper timing was vital, because the reinforcement of Pickens and the evacuation of Sumter had to take place simultaneously, or nearly so. The reason was plain. The moment it became known that Fort Pickens had been reinforced, Fort Sumter would be attacked. Conversely, if Sumter were given up prematurely, the triumphant Confederates might storm the Gulf fort before it could be made safe. The expedition to Pensacola therefore would have to leave hurriedly so as to reach its destination ahead of the day when Anderson would be foodless—April 15, according to Fox's report. The earliest day on which the ships could sail was April 6, and they should arrive not later than the seventeenth. This was close, but not too close, for if Anderson could maintain himself till the fifteenth, he could do so a day or two longer. The garrison might go hungry, but it would not starve.[35]

One of the most vexing parts of the scheme was the outfitting and manning of the Sumter expedition. It would have to present a warlike aspect, yet be too weak to carry out its announced mission. Furthermore, a commander had to be found who inspired confidence, was known to be a fighter, but would not fight. This delicate task was left to Seward, on whose cleverness and discretion Lincoln depended; nor was Lincoln anxious to learn all the arrangements of his Secretary, whose love for intrigue might lead to embarrassing entanglements.

On April 1 the plan began to unfold itself. On that day Lincoln had Seward notify the Confederate Commissioners officially that the evacuation of Sumter no longer was a certainty—but the news was given to them with a wink of the eye. No supplies would be sent without previous notice to the Charleston authorities and it was hinted that, in spite of outward appearances, the promise given by Lamon would be kept.

M. J. Crawford, one of the Confederate Commissioners, immediately wired this latest turnabout to his government:

I am authorized to say that this Government will not undertake to supply Sumter without notice to you. My opinion is that the President . . . intends to shift the responsibility [for vacating the fort] upon Major Anderson by suffering him to be starved out. Would it not be well to aid in this by cutting off all supplies?[36]

Crawford probably gave no thought to the possibility that the opinion he had expressed might have been inspired by Lincoln's wily Secretary of State.

Aside from the factual information and Crawford's own advice in his dispatch, it artfully conveyed two suggestions. For one thing, inasmuch as Sumter was not to be supplied without previous notice to the Southern authorities, hostile action on their part could be safely postponed. This would give Lincoln time to fasten his grip on Fort Pickens. The second item, that Anderson was being allowed to approach starvation, would in all probability be brought to his attention and would weaken his will to hold out. Crawford's gratuitous recommendation to cut off supplies from Sumter fitted well into the President's design.

Five days after this dispatch had been sent, the Charleston authorities received another telegram from Washington which threatened to undo the effect of Crawford's message. It stated positively that Anderson would not be withdrawn, but would be furnished

with supplies. The telegram was signed "A Friend."[37]
The bewildered officials demanded clarification, to be
signed by a man of known responsibility. A reply
arrived promptly. The man of known responsibility
proved to be James E. Harvey, a journalist who,
though of Southern birth, was high in the confidence
of the Washington government. To muddy the waters
further, Harvey followed this wire with a second, contradictory to the first:

Orders issued for withdrawal of Anderson's command.
Scott declares it military necessity. This is private.[38]

The message was confirmed by another saying that
efforts were being made to reconsider the withdrawal,
but they would fail, and by still another stating that no
definite decision had yet been reached. It would have
been a miracle if this barrage of contradictory advices
had not left the Confederate authorities in a state of
mental paralysis. In this way it had been made doubly
sure that for the time being no decisive action on their
part need be apprehended.

A Washington telegraph operator became suspicious
of Harvey's dispatches and promptly informed the
Secretary of the Navy, who hastened to acquaint the
Cabinet with what seemed a treasonable act. He was
astonished and disappointed when his disclosure did
not "elicit any action," and was completely dum-
founded when he learned that, instead of being pun-
ished, Harvey had been appointed American minister
to Portugal.[39] "There was general disapprobation," he
wrote, "except by the President (who avoided the ex-

pression of any opinion) and by Mr. Seward."[40] If the entire Cabinet, including the astute Welles, had been so neatly hoodwinked, Lincoln had reason to believe that the Confederate government likewise would fail to suspect who had sponsored these confusing telegrams, or why they had been sent.

On or about March 20, while Lincoln's preparations for swapping Fort Sumter for a reinforced Fort Pickens were still in their initial stages, he attempted a shrewd side play. He would offer Virginia a deal: if her convention, which had voted to remain in the Union, but was still in session, were to adjourn *sine die,* he would give up Fort Sumter. This was not too great a sacrifice, since he was ready to give it up anyway. He therefore invited George W. Summers, a leading Virginia Unionist, to Washington for a conference. Summers hesitated, and on April 2 Lincoln sent a trusted messenger to Richmond, who returned on April 4 with John B. Baldwin, another Union sympathizer. Baldwin was brought to the White House, and Lincoln held a supersecret conference with him in a locked bedroom. To Lincoln's surprise the Virginian received the proposition coldly, expressing belief that the convention would adjourn only after the evacuation of Fort Sumter was a *fait accompli.* In any event, adjournment would not mean much, as another convention could be called on short notice. What discouraged Lincoln especially was Baldwin's assertion that if shooting should develop at Fort Sumter, no matter who started it, Virginia would go out of the Union at once. When Lincoln heard this, he became excited.

"Why was I not told this a week ago?" he exclaimed.
"You have come too late."[41]

This meeting, unknown at the time even to Lincoln's private secretaries, but later confirmed by both
participants,[42] presents a puzzle. First of all, what
did Lincoln hope to achieve by putting forth a proposition which was so clearly unacceptable? He did not
have to be told that the delegates would scarcely be
naïve enough to vote for it on the strength of a mere
promise, or that adjournments are not necessarily final.
He knew that he was not dealing with political ama-
teurs.

The most persuasive explanation is that Lincoln,
having already decided on a withdrawal from Sumter,
intended to get a high price for it. If his ideas worked
out, the garrison would leave without fighting, and he
could collect a political debt from Virginia. It is hard
to see how he could have lost anything by his offer.

Another enigma is Lincoln's excited exclamation,
"Why was I not told this a week ago? You have come
too late." These words followed Baldwin's statement
that Virginia would secede if either side began shooting. Why was April 4 too late, when whatever was in
Lincoln's mind had been practicable a week earlier?

Lincoln confided to Baldwin that his strongest sup-
porters would no longer allow him to withdraw from
Fort Sumter. This no doubt was true, but it was not
the whole truth. It was true insofar as on the same day
Lincoln had been conferring with several Northern
governors, to whom Baldwin had been introduced.
All the governors entertained decidedly belligerent
ideas and might well have delivered an ultimatum to

the President. The reason for their presence in Washington has never been revealed, but it is believed that Lincoln had invited them to tell them about the relief expedition to Charleston, and to find out how they would react to a call for militia, in case he should issue one. Their favorable, perhaps enthusiastic response very likely was based on the condition that he would stop his efforts at compromising, and that a voluntary surrender of Fort Sumter would lose him their backing. Yet when Lincoln informed Baldwin that he was not free to give up Sumter for this reason he was not entirely frank. His main reason was the uncertainty of the situation at Pensacola. His scheme of yielding Fort Sumter hinged on the assumption that Fort Pickens remained in Federal possession, and this issue was still hanging fire; but this was a secret he could not disclose to anybody, least of all to the governors or to Baldwin. What had caused his sudden excitement was surprise and dismay at the reported weakening of Union sentiment in the Old Dominion state. If Virginia went out with the first shot, what about the warlike instructions he had given to Colonel Brown and to the reckless Porter who was in command of the convoy? If hotheaded Porter rushed unbridled into the face of the Pensacola harbor batteries, as he was apt to do (and subsequently did), and Brown "inflicted all damage in his power," might not the dreaded war start in Florida?

A week ago, on the twenty-eighth, an easy solution had been in sight, for reinforcement of Fort Pickens had then seemed imminent. But the next day Lincoln had become alarmed and had decided on the new plan, which involved expeditions to both disputed forts, one in earnest, the other a sham. In the interim the governors had demanded that he stiffen his attitude, and he had intimated to them the possible use of militia. No wonder he lamented that Baldwin had come a week too late.[43]

Fortunately, the Virginia deal had been no more than a daring speculation. Nothing had been lost by its miscarriage; the main issue had not been touched. It appeared that Fort Pickens could yet be strengthened before Fort Sumter had to surrender. In neither place did it seem likely that a shot would be fired in anger. The prospects for continued peace therefore still looked favorable.

3

The Maneuvers Miscarry

THE HOPEFULNESS which pervaded the White House on April 4 was suddenly dispelled by a rude shock. The cause was a letter from Anderson which threatened to shatter Lincoln's peace plan beyond redemption. The letter, dated April 1, ended with this paragraph:

I told Mr. Fox that if I placed the command on short allowance I could make the provisions last until after the 10th of this month; but as I have received no instructions . . . it has not been done. If the governor [Pickens] permits me to send off the laborers we will have rations enough to last us about one week longer.[1]

These were grim tidings indeed. Lincoln's schedule was based on the assumption that the fort could sustain itself comfortably till the fifteenth, and uncomfortably till the seventeenth, the day on which the reinforcements were due at Pensacola. Anderson's letter showed this assumption to be wrong.

That the President was greatly disturbed by this unexpected blow is attested by a note in the memoirs of John A. Dahlgren, chief ordnance officer of the Washington Navy Yard. The entry is written in the third person: "At Lincoln's request Dahlgren called again early the next day [April 5]. He found the President 'ill at ease, and not self-possessed.' "[2] In view of Lincoln's well-known equanimity, it is significant that a man who had only recently become acquainted with him noticed his profound agitation and made a note of it.

Who was responsible for this egregious blunder? Not Anderson. While talking to Fox on March 21, he claimed to have distinctly tied the date of April 15 to an immediate reduction of the rations.[3] As ill luck would have it, the harassed commandant had omitted all mention of this premise in his report.[4] Nevertheless, his veracity was above reproach. He was an officer with thirty years of honorable service to his credit, and it is unthinkable that he would have endangered his record by a false statement, especially as it involved a man who had the President's ear, and recently had been entrusted with an important mission.

Was Lincoln responsible for the misunderstanding? No. If such an essential factor in his reckoning had been brought to his attention, he hardly would have forgotten or overlooked it. By indirection therefore the blunder must be laid at Fox's door, although there is no definite proof of his guilt. Apparently he had reported only orally to Lincoln after his return from Fort Sumter; at least nothing in writing has been found in the *Official Records* or in his private correspondence. Not until four years later did he make any reference at all to this matter, and then he did not touch on the disputed point. All he said was:

I found the garrison getting short of supplies, and it was agreed that I might report that the 15th of April, at noon, would be the period beyond which the fort could not be held unless supplies were furnished.[5]

Fox apparently was guilty of nothing worse than either negligence or forgetfulness; yet one must wonder what would have happened if he had reported Anderson's statement in full, or if Anderson had stressed in his official report that his estimate was contingent on an immediate cut in the daily food rations.

No matter who was responsible, Anderson's letter blasted all hopes that he could sustain himself until the fifteenth. The new deadline, as he vaguely indicated, would be April 10. Adding two foodless days would mark the twelfth as the absolute limit of his staying power. Lincoln's elaborate timetable thus was thrown out of kilter and had to be advanced by fully five days. Anderson's expectation that he could hold out till the fifteenth, made on March 21, hinged on the condition that the rations would be reduced at once. A reduction, to Anderson, meant cutting them in half, as he was to demonstrate in the next few days. When he wrote his letter on April 1, ten days had gone by since Fox's departure. If during the interval the reduction had been in effect, it would have saved five days' food supplies; but since "it had not been done," as he observed in muted censure, these days had been irretrievably lost, and had to be deducted from his original end date of the fifteenth. It was that simple, or rather it would have been that simple had not two additional x's crept into the equation. One was whether in the meantime the Confederates had refused to remove his laborers, as he seemed to fear; another was whether the authorities had followed Crawford's suggestion of April 1 to stop sending food to the fort. Anderson himself appeared anxious only about his laborers, and his apprehension was well grounded, because Governor Pickens did disallow his request to ship them off. On the other hand, he evidently did not expect a stoppage of his food purchases, which likewise proved a correct forecast. But Lincoln thought differently. Most likely, he believed the Confederates would take Crawford's advice and immediately cut off Anderson's means of prolonging his resistance. If so, the garrison would be entirely out of food even prior to the tenth.

This speculation, founded on more guesswork than Lincoln could have wished for, led him to the conclusion that Anderson would be forced to surrender by April 12 at the latest, at which time the men would have gone without nourishment for two, perhaps three days. Fort Pickens therefore had to be made secure not by the seventeenth, the day heretofore set, but as near to the twelfth as possible, and with whatever troops were available. Luckily, the outlook for bringing this about was promising; a messenger could reach Pensacola by rail in four or five days, which allowed a fair margin of safety.

Considering the meager data at his disposal, Lincoln's estimate proved remarkably close. In a letter written Friday, April 5, Anderson announced that he would have to abandon his post "very early next week," or else stay on without food.[6] The very early part of the next week would end on Tuesday the ninth, which would make the eleventh or twelfth the day of surrender. The President had not missed the mark by much, if at all. He might have felt somewhat easier had he known that one of his fears did not materialize. While the Montgomery government had forced Anderson to keep his laborers, Beauregard had not complied with an order from the Confederate Secretary of War to stop forthwith sending provisions to the fort. This order, dated April 2, read in part as follows:

> The . . . vacillations of the Washington Government make it imperative that . . . further . . . courtesies . . . to Major Anderson . . . must cease; . . . signify . . . to Major Anderson that all communication with the city . . . for any purpose of supply is absolutely prohibited; and . . . at the earliest moment practicable you will make your . . . enforcement . . . as rigid as all the means at your command and the most watchful vigilance can secure.[7]

It is almost inconceivable that any officer would dare disobey an order styled so plainly and so urgently. Yet disobey it Beauregard did. For a week longer he continued to provide Sumter with fresh meat and vegetables.[8] Anderson once had been Beauregard's instructor at West Point, and from a human point of view the behavior of the Confederate general is understandable; yet history records few cases of amenity which have incurred more portentous consequences.

Inasmuch as it was now plain that Anderson could not possibly hold out till April 17, Porter's expedition to the Gulf, which was not due there until that day, had lost its importance. If Fort Pickens were to be reinforced in time to fit into the general scheme, it would have to be accomplished by the eleventh or the twelfth.

Accurate timing was now essential, because all operations had to converge on April 12. In this respect the Fort Pickens problem was not troublesome; it required only that a messenger arrive there at precisely the right time. It would not do to send him off at once after receipt of Anderson's letter, for in that case he would arrive on the eighth or the ninth, which was too soon. Anderson would not be ready to yield at this early date, nor could the commander at Pensacola be restrained for three or four days without giving away Lincoln's plan. The messenger would have to deliver the instructions on April 11 or 12, neither sooner nor later. This meant he must leave Washington on the seventh.

One may well question why, in the absence of an agent at the Gulf, the original order had not been sent by rail instead of by the slow and uncertain sea route. Rail communication had been more feasible in March than in April; and even though a written dispatch had been intercepted, if it had contained nothing but a warning that the order then on its way by sea was to be obeyed implicitly, very little would have been risked. Fort Pickens would have been reinforced by April 1, in which case Lincoln could have evacuated Fort Sumter without loss of prestige. With this chief obstacle to peace out of the way, the specter of war would have been banished.

In contrast to the situation at Pensacola, the one at Charleston required very careful handling. Since Anderson's April 1 letter had brought the crisis considerably nearer than had been believed, the relief fleet, so far readied only conditionally, had to be given definite sailing orders. Its arrival at Charleston was therefore set for April 11,[9] to coincide with that of the messenger at the Gulf. Immediately following receipt of the news from Anderson, Fox was summoned to the White House and directed to fit out the expedition for departure at the appropriate time. On protesting that the time was too short for proper preparations, he was given the cryptic reply that he would best fulfill his duty to his country by making the attempt,[10] even if it should fail. The significance of this remark escaped Fox, for he made no record of it. It was to be recalled to his mind before long.

On the same day Fox was handed his official appointment from Secretary of War Cameron. The document read:

It having been determined to succor Fort Sumter you have been selected for this important duty. Ac-

cordingly you will take charge of the transports provided in New York, . . . and endeavor . . . to deliver
the subsistence. If you are opposed . . . you are . . .
to report the fact to the Senior Naval officer off the
harbor, who will be instructed by the Secretary of the
Navy to use his entire force to open a passage, when
you will, if possible, effect an entrance and place both
the troops and supplies in Fort Sumter.[11]

There was nothing equivocal about this order; if executed it would usher in civil war.

On the third of April Fox had written to a friend:
"My expedition is ordered to be got ready, but I doubt
if we shall get off. Delay, indecision, obstacles."[12] He
did not suspect that the delays and obstacles were
intentional, and that the expedition would not have
been ordered out at all but for the confusion at the
Gulf, and certainly not so early as it was but for Anderson's unwelcome message. The normal sailing time
from New York to Charleston was three days, therefore Fox could not be allowed to leave before the
eighth.

Lincoln himself pictured the condition of affairs at
this juncture in these words:

. . . To now re-inforce Fort Pickens [by Porter's ex-
pedition], before a crisis would be reached at Fort
Sumter was impossible—rendered so by the near ex-
haustion of provisions in the latter-named Fort. In
precaution against such a conjecture, the government
had, a few days before, commenced preparing an

expedition . . . to relieve Fort Sumter, which expedition was intended to be . . . used, or not, according to circumstances. The strongest anticipated case, for using it, was now presented; and it was resolved to send it forward.[13]

To those unaware of the reasons behind the purposeful delay it must have seemed almost incredible that despite Anderson's desperate need, the relief fleet was not rushed posthaste to its destination. Yet the Secretary of the Navy waited a full day before he ordered Fox's ships to rendezvous off Charleston harbor, and then they were directed not to arrive until the morning of the eleventh.[14] If this looked like a leisurely proceeding, the remainder of the arrangements were business-like enough. Captain Samuel Mercer of the *Powhatan,* who was to command the navy part of the enterprise, received precise instructions from Welles how to co-operate with Fox, who had been put in supreme charge of the operation. Mercer's orders were as belligerent as those given to Fox by the Secretary of War:

The primary object of the expedition is to provision Fort Sumter.

. . . Should the authorities at Charleston . . . attempt to prevent the . . . vessels . . . from entering the harbor . . . peaceably, . . . you will protect [them]; . . . in case of resistance . . . a reenforcement of the garrison will also be attempted . . . under the supervision of the War Department, which has charge of the expedi-

tion. The expedition has been intrusted to Captain
G. V. Fox, with whom you will put yourself in communication, and cooperate with him to accomplish
and carry into effect its object.[15]

For reasons which he never was asked to explain,
Mercer followed neither the letter nor the spirit of the
last sentence. If he had, subsequent events might have
taken a sharply different course.

The President's next task was a delicate one, and
stood in sharp contrast to his overt warlike preparations. He had to issue discreet instructions to Anderson to maintain his position until April 11, or a day
beyond, and thereafter to surrender. Lincoln lost no
time about it. Immediately after reading Anderson's
report, he drafted a skillfully worded reply. It had two
aims: Anderson must be induced to yield, but not earlier than the appointed time; and the Confederates
must be kept from prematurely firing on him. The
message was meant for them as well, because Lincoln
conjectured, rightly as it proved, that they would open
and read the official Northern mail. The difficulty was
to phrase the letter in such a way as to avoid losing
the support of the governors, should the Secessionists
choose to make it public. Furthermore, Anderson
had to be made to understand that Sumter must be
given up, and the only ground which would justify
his action to everyone—the governors, the war
party and himself—was military necessity. This necessity would not arise until the eleventh or twelfth.

Lincoln no doubt pondered long over this order

before he asked the Secretary of War to sign it. The order began:

Your letter of the 1st instant occasions some anxiety to the President.

On the information of Captain Fox he had supposed you could hold out till the 15th instant without any great inconvenience; and had prepared an expedition to relieve you before that period.[16]

An old soldier surely would not consider going on half rations a great inconvenience. The President hoped that Anderson would understand that he was to employ this expedient at once, and thereby stretch his food supply. Lincoln was acting on the supposition that no provisions had reached the fort since April 1, and he was therefore concerned that Anderson might surrender too soon, possibly as early as the ninth. By hoarding his provisions he might be able to hold out till the eleventh or twelfth.

This part of the letter, which arrived on the seventh, Anderson did understand, although the shutting off of supplies, which Beauregard at last had put into effect on the same day, may have influenced his decision. At any rate, the rations of the garrison now were cut in half.[17] The message next indicated the need of holding out till the eleventh or twelfth, putting special emphasis on these two days:

Hoping still that you will be able to sustain yourself till the 11th or 12th instant, the expedition will go forward; and, finding your flag flying, will attempt to provision you, and, in case the effort is resisted, will endeavor also to re-enforce you. You will therefore hold out, if possible, till the arrival of the expedition.

Anderson was thus given the choice of two days on which to give up the fort, and simultaneously he was instructed to wait for the arrival of the expedition. The implication was unmistakable—the two events would coincide. The rest of the message made its principal purpose still clearer:

It is not, however, the intention of the President to subject your command to any danger or hardship beyond what, in your judgment, would be usual in military life, and he has entire confidence that you will act as becomes a patriot and soldier, under all circumstances. Whenever, if at all, in your judgment, to save yourself and command, a capitulation becomes a necessity, you are authorized to make it.

Respectfully yours,
Simon Cameron
Secretary of War

Anderson knew, as every army officer did, that in a case of this kind authorization was superfluous. Capitulation through necessity was the recognized privilege, not to say duty, of any commander. Had he studied the letter carefully, he would have deduced what this needless emphasis was trying to convey to him, especially as he was assured that his surrender was not incompatible with patriotism. It was impossible for Lincoln to intimate that the relief expedition would not perform its announced objective; but the words "the expedition will attempt to provision you," and "will endeavor to re-enforce you" were hints that the promise of help was not a definite one. Anderson was told to hold out only till the arrival of the fleet; beyond that he had no instructions, but its conduct should give him his final clue. Steps had been taken to make certain that the fleet would not go into action.

As to the Confederates, Lincoln's letter to Anderson also would serve its purpose. From it they would learn the fort was about to be abandoned; why then use force? Once more, however, Lincoln's inattention to details took its toll. He could have avoided relying on Anderson's ingenuity to read between the lines, if he had made previous arrangements to communicate with the isolated fort. Anderson himself expressed a veiled reproach that this had not been done, when he wrote to the War Department on April 5: "I am sure that I shall not be left without instructions even though they may be confidential."[18]

There is reason to believe Lincoln did make a belated attempt to give the distracted commander confidential orders. R. S. Chew, a clerk in the State Department, arrived in Charleston on April 8, and handed Governor Pickens a message from Lincoln, stating that an attempt for peacefully provisioning Fort Sumter was in the offing. Chew was accompanied by Captain Theodore Talbot, one of Anderson's officers, who was returning from Washington. Relations between the two governments had become so strained, however, that Talbot was not permitted to rejoin his command.[19] Lincoln may have expected this, because he had improvised another device to instruct Anderson. He ordered the message made out in quadruplicate and sent the extra copies to Sumter "by other methods," as Nicolay and Hay put it.[20] What these methods were, they did not divulge; it did not matter, because none of the copies reached its destination.

An intriguing part of Talbot's mission is that he carried with him a secret message to Anderson; unfortunately, it is not known what it was. Nicolay and Hay made no allusion to it, and the *Official Records* disclose only that Talbot returned to Washington still carrying a sealed letter which had been entrusted to him by the President in person at the start of his trip.[21]

The significance of this communication lies in the fact that it was sent at all. What Lincoln had written must necessarily have been either additional or contradictory to some of the instructions he had issued to Anderson in Cameron's April 4 letter. A third possibility which has been suggested, that the President only advised Anderson of his message to Governor Pickens, need not be seriously considered, for in that case it could have been sent openly. To draw further inferences is risky; but if the contents of this letter should ever become known, they may put an end to all speculations on the mysteries of the Sumter affair.

The Confederates erred grievously in stopping the delivery of Lincoln's communication. By doing so they threw away the last chance for a peaceable settlement of the national issues. What Lincoln had written could not possibly have been detrimental to their cause. If Anderson had been ordered to hold out, it would not have mattered, because they were ready to subdue him with guns; but if he had been ordered to surrender at a given date, the main obstacle to the preservation of peace would have been removed. In refusing to let Lincoln's letter go through, Governor Pickens added a crowning blunder to a career already heavily studded with proofs of poor judgment.

Cameron's dispatch to Anderson had been hurriedly mailed on April 4[22] to assure its arrival a few hours before Chew's delivery of Lincoln's message to the South Carolina governor on the eighth. The virtually simultaneous arrivals of the two, together with an identical notice in both regarding peaceable provisioning of the fort, were to allay any suspicions of double-dealing which might bring about a headlong attack. But even though Pickens might be inclined toward making one, he would first have to consult Montgomery, and that took time.

The day after Chew's arrival the Charleston authorities stopped mail service to the fort,[23] but in all probability the governor had read Lincoln's letter prior to giving his order. In fact, he would have been remiss in his duty had he done otherwise. Evidence that the privacy of letters was no longer respected may be found in advices which Beauregard had received. His superiors intimated that he was, "while allowing Major Anderson to receive his mails, to exercise such instructive discretion as will secure the ends in view."[24] In other words, Beauregard was to seize Anderson's mail and turn it over to the authorities for perusal before forwarding it.

That the governor did read Lincoln's letter is also

indicated by an entry in the diary of Mrs. Chesnut, wife of a prominent Charleston politician and a member of the governor's staff. She wrote on April 8: "Now they have intercepted a letter from him [Anderson] urging them to let him surrender. . . ."[25] Mrs. Chesnut had got her information slightly twisted. Together with Lincoln's order, one of Anderson's letters to the War Department had been intercepted, but it said nothing about surrendering; it was Lincoln's letter, signed by Cameron, which did. This, however, was unimportant. What was important was that the Confederates, as Lincoln had figured, were aware that Sumter was about to pass into their hands without fighting.

The full text of the message to the governor ran like this:

I am directed by the President of the United States to notify you to expect an attempt will be made to supply Fort Sumter with provisions only, and that, if such attempt be not resisted, no effort to throw in men, arms or ammunition, will be made, without further notice, or in case of an attack upon the Fort.[26]

It was a queer communication. Superficially it sounded conciliatory, but the closing sentence was anything but pacific. No self-respecting government could accept a proposition couched in such casuistic language. What was meant by "without further notice"? Under the terms of this letter, boats could land at Fort Sumter, unload their provisions and then give

notice that men and ammunition would follow immediately. The action would be completed before the
Confederates could do anything about it.

Lincoln's proposal was so preposterous because he
could not afford to have it accepted. Both the reinforcement of Fort Pickens and Anderson's surrender
had been scheduled for the eleventh or twelfth, and
until then everything had to be held in *status quo*. If
Sumter were provisioned prematurely, the Confederates might counter by taking the Gulf fort, which Lincoln wanted to hold. He certainly did not want to
exchange it for the one at Charleston, which he could
not have held indefinitely.

The more one studies Lincoln's letter to Governor
Pickens, the more one must marvel at its adroitness,
for it met three of the four conditions in his over-all
plan. The peace party was assuaged by the assurance
that provisioning was the sole purpose of the expedition, while the presence of warships should please
the warmongers. Furthermore, the letter threw the
Confederates into temporary confusion, thereby gain-
ing for the President the few days' time which he
so desperately needed. For the fourth fundamental
point he depended on the hint given to Anderson that
his surrender was being expected. The hope was justified that a satisfactory culmination was near.

Lincoln could have dispensed with the fleet if he
really intended to provision Fort Sumter. An unarmed
cargo boat could have been sent off on short notice;
if the Confederates attacked it, they would be "firing
on bread." But the little fort had long ceased to be of

military importance; it had become a political pawn
in a game in which the stakes were of the highest.

Trying to force Anderson into line with the general
design had been difficult; to do the same with Fox
was more so. Fox had to reach Charleston on the
eleventh or twelfth; the tenth would be too early, for
it might incite the Confederates into attacking Fort
Pickens. The thirteenth would be too late, for according to Lincoln's calculations Anderson would have
capitulated by that time. Moreover, the delay in forwarding the expedition could not be explained without disclosing the reason for it. In addition, Fox could
not be told why his impatience to get under way was
being stifled; still more delicate handling was needed
to prevent him from entering the harbor, yet leave him
under the impression that delivery of the provisions
was his primary duty.

Even under normal conditions it would have required all of Lincoln's ingenuity to carry this complex
plan to fruition, but conditions were anything but
normal. One of the greatest hindrances was that no
one but Seward was allowed to learn all the ins and
outs of the project, and even he could never be quite
sure what was in the President's mind. Welles had
been left entirely in the dark. Like everyone else, he
was led to believe that Lincoln actually intended to
supply Fort Sumter and, incredibly, he had not been
told anything about Porter's mission to the Gulf, although it pertained to his department. And so, with
all threads running through Lincoln's fingers, and he

alone weaving the pattern, his task had grown to almost superhuman proportions.

Fox boarded the troopship *Baltic* in New York on the sixth and wrote hopefully to his wife that he expected to sail the next morning. His expectations were not fulfilled because, as he observed disgustedly, "every effort was made by some strong hand to delay the expedition."[27] The first effects of the secret maneuvers against him were becoming manifest.

Still, all did not look black. He had succeeded in hiring, under army sponsorship, three tugs to carry most of the supplies and troops into the harbor. This was good news for, despite orders from his immediate superior and those of Secretary Welles to the commander of the fleet, the prudent Fox had no intention of letting the warships cross the bar, allowing the Navy to take the lion's share of the credit. Another piece of good luck was that his expedition had been allotted the *Powhatan,* considered the best ship in the home fleet. She was the only vessel equipped with the tools which Fox proposed to use: boats sufficiently large for heavy loads, enough skilled sailors to handle them, and fighting launches to fend off Confederate patrol boats inside the harbor. The *Powhatan,* Fox declared, was "the main portion, the fighting portion, of our expedition."[28] The need for her presence was further accentuated by the fact that she was to be the flagship, and that all Welles's orders to the other ships centered around her.[29]

Fox doubtlessly would have resigned then and there,

if he had known that the *Powhatan* was not to be his
after all. She had been kidnapped by Porter, who,
fortified by an order over Lincoln's signature, had
chosen her to carry him to Pensacola on his reinforcement expedition. It was either one of the most fan-
tastic mix-ups or else one of the cleverest intrigues in
the annals of the war.

Welles's order to Mercer, captain of the *Powhatan*
and senior officer of the fleet, stated that the War Department had charge of the expedition, and that the
man heading it was Fox, "with whom you will put
yourself in communication and cooperate with him"
to accomplish the object of the expedition. When
Mercer received instructions from the President—
without Welles's knowledge—to relinquish the *Powhatan* to Porter, one might have expected him to obey
the Secretary's specific order and co-operate with Fox
by acquainting him with this radical change in arrangements. Fox was within easy reach, as the *Baltic*
had anchored in New York harbor only a few miles
distant. Mercer, however, did nothing of the sort. He
even failed to inform Welles of having relinquished
the *Powhatan* to Porter, probably in the belief that the
informing had been done by Lincoln. Instead he surrendered Welles's order to the captain of the *Harriet
Lane*, then also in New York harbor, with directions
to deliver it after his arrival at Charleston to the rank-
ing naval officer there, whoever he might be. Welles's
order had said nothing about the detachment of the
Powhatan because he was not aware of it, but Mercer
was, and when forwarding the Secretary's instructions,
quite properly attached to them a personal note of his

own that carried this all-important intelligence.[30] It was this note which by all means should have gone straight to Fox. Being unofficial, it was not subject to navy regulations, and there was no excuse to detour it via Charleston, especially as any delay in its delivery was sure to wreak havoc with Fox's expedition. Nevertheless, Mercer dispatched it in this roundabout way by the *Harriet Lane* without even, so far as appears from the record and from future events, ordering its delivery to Fox. Mercer's action is the more astounding as he was fully acquainted with Welles's directions to all captains of the fleet, which ended with this sentence: "On the morning of the 11th instant . . . you will report to Captain Mercer of the *Powhatan* . . . Should he not be there, you will await his arrival."[31] How could an officer of Mercer's standing and experience fail to visualize the confusion which was bound to follow now that neither he nor the *Powhatan* would arrive at all? Should he not have realized that this confusion would be doubly confounded if Fox, the commander of the expedition, were kept in ignorance of the changed dispositions?

Some inkling of who was responsible for this mischief may be gleaned from a report which A. H. Foote, commandant of the Brooklyn Navy Yard, sent to Welles on April 6. It appeared that on April 1 Porter had delivered to him in person a presidential order which was so extraordinary that he must have stared at it with unbelieving eyes. "You will fit out the *Powhatan* without delay," it read. "Lieutenant Porter will relieve Captain Mercer in command of her. She is bound on secret service." A message sent directly from the President to a captain instead of through the Secretary of the Navy was curious enough, but what followed was downright staggering. "You will under no circumstance," Lincoln had written, "communicate to the Navy Department the fact that she [the *Powhatan*] is fitting out."[32] In other words, Foote was ordered to conspire against the Cabinet officer under whom he was serving and, what was still more amazing, was given the impression that he enjoyed the President's confidence while Welles did not. Tradition made him rebel against this breach of military usage, but all he could do was to give Porter some uneasy moments by demanding telegraphic confirmation from Welles before releasing the vessel.[33] If he had insisted, the ensuing scene in Washington would have put a farce comedy to shame; but Porter, after a two-hour verbal onslaught during which he shot off every argument in his armory, managed to talk Foote out of following his inclination.[34] Thus the path of the conspirators was cleared of its most menacing obstacle.

Stunned as he was already, the artless navy captain soon had another matter to worry about. Prior to the departure of the *Powhatan*, Captain Meigs, Lieutenant Porter and Captain Mercer held a conference in his own quarters to which he was not invited, much to his ill-concealed displeasure.[35] The three officers, however, knew what they were doing; they wanted no witnesses, because it was there that they agreed on the circuitous route by which they were to let Fox receive Welles's order to Mercer.[36] As to the latter's private note, they would see that Fox did not receive it in time to profit by its contents.

The *why* of their decision thus to hamstring the commander of the expedition offers a field for speculation. Did the navy officers take offense at being subordinated to the War Department? But Meigs, one of the three, was an army captain. Did the senior navy officer resent that the expedition was under the command of a civilian, who had left the Navy in 1856 and, while in the service, had never risen above the grade of acting lieutenant?[37] This argument might have appealed to Mercer, but could not have impressed the other two officers, whose ranks were about on the same level as that of Fox. The most likely explanation is that the unsuspecting Mercer was being manipulated by Meigs and Porter, who were known to be special protégés of Seward. They had taken orders from him ever since he had come into office, were deep in his confidence, and knew that he was determined to wreck Fox's expedition by fair means or foul.

On April 6 official news reached Washington that Fort Pickens had not been reinforced.[38] The dispatch arrived just in time to furnish an excuse for bundling off a messenger, who would have taken off anyway the next day. John L. Worden, a navy lieutenant who someday would become famous as the commander of the *Monitor,* was sent by rail to Pensacola, with a message containing instructions to strengthen the fort at once with whatever troops were on hand. He left in the morning of the seventh and, traveling day and night, should reach the Gulf on the eleventh or twelfth at the latest.[39] Since Anderson had been ordered to hold out this long, the outlook was promising that, in spite of all mishaps, the President's hopes would be fulfilled. Seward was in high spirits. He wrote to Justice Campbell, a Confederate go-between, with cheery confidence: "Faith as to Sumter fully kept—wait and see."[40]

While Worden was en route to the Gulf, Fox's relief fleet was gradually assembling off Charleston harbor. The *Harriet Lane* had sailed out of New York on April 8; the *Baltic,* with Fox aboard, followed the next day. From Norfolk the *Pawnee* departed on the ninth, the *Pocahontas* on the tenth. Hampered by a heavy gale, the tugs never arrived, but the remaining vessels rendezvoused off the bar in the early morning of the twelfth, with the exception of the *Pocahontas,* which did not show up until the morning of the thirteenth. On the whole the timing had been excellent. The condition of the ships, however, showed that the mission was a stage affair despite its awe-inspiring appearance. The *Pawnee* and the *Harriet Lane* were insufficiently manned and their boats were unfit for carrying loads.[41] Two weeks before, Fox had been willing to overlook these shortcomings, for he had written to Blair that "the *Baltic's* ten boats will hold all the men and the Provisions";[42] but now he found that not one of her boats was seaworthy. If a man had fallen overboard, he could not have been saved. The troops were raw recruits, most of whom never had handled a gun.[43] The war vessels, which Fox did not intend to use in any case, could not have entered the harbor without undue risks. In daylight they would have had to brave the shore batteries, and at night they could not have avoided the shoals since all buoys had been removed. Anderson was almost out of oil, hence could not provide light signals; and no pilots could be obtained to steer the ships through the treacherous channel. On top of all this, the Confederates had installed Drummond searchlights, making a stealthy approach in the dark impossible. Small boats, had they been on hand, would have been at the mercy of the Confederate patrol ships and the concentrated fire of the shore guns. The venture would have been hazardous even if the tugs and the *Powhatan's* boats had been available, but without them Fox was commanding a ghost expedition which had no chance of succeeding. In his official report Captain J. P. Gillis of the *Pocahontas* told of a conversation with Anderson after the fort had surrendered. Anderson, Gillis wrote, considered it "very providential" that the attempt to throw supplies into Sumter had not been made, "as it could not have been successfully executed. . . ."[44]

When the *Baltic* reached the entrance of Charleston harbor at 3:00 A.M. of the twelfth, she found only the *Harriet Lane* there. Some very peculiar things then began to happen. "At 6 a. m.," Fox reported, "the *Pawnee* was seen standing in. I boarded her and informed her commander [Captain C. S. Rowan] of my orders to offer to send in provisions, and asked him to stand in to the bar with me." Rowan refused. "He replied that his orders required him to . . . await the *Powhatan*. . . ."[45] Rowan indulged in this piece of impudence, although he later admitted having opened Welles's official dispatch and therefore knew that he was speaking to his commander.[46] Undoubtedly he

had also read Mercer's private note advising him that
the *Powhatan* would not show up, but this information
he kept to himself.

Rowan's own report is not without interest, although
it throws little light on his strange behavior. It does
show definitely that he had read Welles's order: "On
approaching the harbor," he wrote, "a small . . .
steamer approached, which proved to be the *Harriet
Lane*. A boat was sent from her with a communication . . . to the senior naval officer present, which I
opened and found to be a . . . dispatch from the Navy
Department, . . . addressed to Captain Samuel
Mercer. . . ."[47] Thus it appears that the captain of
the *Harriet Lane,* following orders, had by-passed
Fox, who was handed the official dispatch later. But
neither in his report nor at any subsequent time did
Rowan mention Mercer's private note; its content has
not been published in the *Official Records,* and still
is unknown. Quite naturally he also neglected to mention his refusal to accompany Fox when ordered to do
so. That Rowan kept Mercer's personal note from the
commander of the expedition until too late to be of any
use to him challenges one's credulity. Fox, in the belief that the *Powhatan* could be expected momentarily,
made his plans accordingly, and thereby sealed Anderson's fate.

Captain Rowan was an officer of high repute. Inasmuch as his order from the Navy Department to await
the arrival of the *Powhatan* had never been revoked,
he may have been, literally speaking, within his rights
in declining to disobey it, although in this case disobedience would seem to have been his proper course.

The captain of the *Harriet Lane*, who had asked for and received a copy of Welles's official instructions, interpreted them more liberally. He "cheerfully accompanied me," Fox recorded.[48]

The firing on Fort Sumter had been going on for several hours, but it was not until the forenoon that the noise and smoke were noticed by the navy men, who were several miles away. Seeing that fighting had begun, Rowan needed no further persuasion to join the other two vessels. Strangely, it was now Fox who evinced no desire to cross the bar. "It was observed," he stated in his report of April 19, "that war had commenced, and therefore the peaceful offer of provisions was void."[49] But was it? Lincoln's letter to Anderson stated that the expedition would attempt to provision the fort if it found its flag still flying. The flag could be seen when the expedition arrived, and it flew for many hours thereafter. Moreover, Fox had been ordered by Secretary of War Cameron "to deliver the subsistence" and, if opposed, to report the fact to the senior naval officer present, who was instructed "to use his entire force to open passage." Mercer had received almost identical instructions from Welles,[50] and they had been read by Rowan, the "senior naval officer present." It was evident that the possibility of an armed outbreak had been foreseen, and directions had been issued in case a "peaceful offer of provisions" should be resisted. According to these orders, not to mention the universal tradition of armed forces in time of war, Fox should have hurried to the scene of the battle and joined it. Why did he not do so?

Whatever was at the bottom of Fox's odd conduct, April 12 passed while the fleet stood idly by, watching Anderson's fire slacken and black clouds of smoke gather over the doomed work. The crews of the warships, seeing their comrades-in-arms battered mercilessly, must have asked themselves why they had come at all.

In the morning of the thirteenth the *Pocahontas* arrived, and her captain now became the senior naval officer. He declared himself ready to force the channel if he could procure a pilot. No pilot being obtainable, he successfully resisted "his strong impulse" to rush in.[51]

During the night of the twelfth, Fox had been willing to send off two small boats, loaded with provisions, but said he was overruled.[52] That he let himself be overruled by his subordinates is hardly credible. The plan probably was dropped because two boatloads could not have been of any consequence, and Fox was pinning his hopes on the *Powhatan's* boats which he believed to be near, and with which he would be in a position to help Anderson on a worth-while scale.

In his report Fox gave vent to his fury at the way he had been stultified:

Feeling sure that the *Powhatan* would arrive during the night [of the twelfth], I stood out . . . and made signals all night. The morning of the 13th, . . . I now learned for the first time that Captain Rowan had received a note from Captain Mercer . . . dated at New York the 6th . . . stating that the *Powhatan* was detached . . . and had sailed for another destination.

I left New York two days afterwards without any intimation of this change.[53]

Surprisingly, Fox did not say whether he had asked Rowan to account for the temporary suppression of Mercer's private note. All he said was that "in justice to itself . . . I trust the Government has sufficient reasons for putting me in the position they have placed me."[54] The thrusts at Lincoln and Seward, although oblique, were unmistakable.

In a letter to his friend Blair, Fox added some acid comments. "You will see that some one determined to utterly extinguish the expedition. I do not think I have deserved this treatment." At the conclusion of his letter his resentment flared up again: "As for our expedition, somebody's influence has made it ridiculous."[55]

Fox had every right to be furious. He had, as he stated, lain in New York harbor for two days after the departure of the *Powhatan*, yet none of the few who knew of it, Lincoln and Seward included, had informed him. Still worse, an officer of his own squadron, who possessed this information, had concealed it from him. Small wonder that he poured out his rage and puzzlement to the man who had recommended him for what at one time had looked like a most promising assignment.

While Fox fumed and fretted, the *Powhatan* was hundreds of miles away on her journey to the Gulf, followed by the wrath of Welles, who had at last found out what had gone on behind his back. Foote, dis-

turbed by the irregularities he had observed, had
defied Lincoln's injunction, and on April 6 had com-
municated with the Secretary.[56] Despite the late hour,
Welles carried his indignation to the White House,
whereupon the President ordered Seward to recall the
Powhatan by wire and turn her over to Fox. But once
again the hands which were pulling the hidden strings
went to work. After his experience with Scott, Lincoln
should have known that, just as an order of a Cabinet
member could not be revoked by a general, a presidential order could not be revoked by anyone but
himself; nevertheless, he directed Seward to sign the
telegram. This gave Porter a way out. He rightly
claimed that the President's order took precedence
over one signed by a Cabinet officer, and merrily kept
on his way.

Seward's attitude is easy to understand. Regarding
Sumter as the only roadblock to peace, he had given
the Southern Commissioners his assurance that it
would be given up, and he was determined to scuttle
Fox's venture. Analyzing Lincoln's part in the trans-
action is more difficult. He declared he had signed
the original order concerning the *Powhatan* without
having read it, and blamed the error on his own carelessness.

Welles was not satisfied. He had taken the precaution of making the President listen while he read his
instructions to Mercer. According to them the *Powhatan* was to be the flagship of the Sumter fleet. Lincoln admitted remembering the incident, but he said
he had forgotten the name of the vessel.[57] However,
he also had signed the warning to Foote to keep the

order for her detachment from Welles, and in this case his explanation that he had not read it was far less convincing, because even a cursory glance at the few lines would have shown him the anomaly to which he was affixing his name. For letting Seward sign the telegram to Porter he offered no explanation at all. It would be more than charitable to ascribe his part in these three closely related transactions to mere carelessness. Even John T. Morse, Jr., one of Lincoln's partisan biographers, scoffed at the President's protestations. "The only excuse which has ever been advanced in behalf of Mr. Lincoln," he wrote, "is that he allowed himself to be led blindfold . . . by Mr. Seward. . . . But such an excuse, even if it can be believed, seems fully as bad as the blunder which it is designed to palliate."[58] If Lincoln really had wanted to stop Porter, the reasonable thing for him to do was to put Porter's recall into the hands of Welles, not into those of Seward. Welles was present, had done the complaining, and the matter pertained strictly to his department. The Secretary of the Navy was meticulous in all he did and, knowing that the original order had been issued by Lincoln, would have insisted on a presidential endorsement. But whether or not Lincoln had been a party to the plot, he was not unhappy about its success. In the absence of the *Powhatan*, Anderson would receive no provisions.

In one of his private letters Fox admitted that he could not "state the facts at this crisis of our affairs without injury to the Govt."[59] What he did do was to address a letter to the President, complaining that the nonappearance of the *Powhatan* had upset his plans.

But Lincoln had subtle ways of soothing hurt feelings. Within a few days Fox found himself promoted to the position of Chief Clerk of the Navy Department; and a short time afterward was appointed Assistant Secretary of the Navy,[60] which not only pleased him, but proved of great benefit to the Northern cause.

In his new and powerful position Fox might have ordered Mercer and Rowan before a board of inquiry. Guilty or not, their conduct called for an investigation, and history would have been served well by their testimonies. Mercer's explanation for his refusal to co-operate with Fox in accordance with Welles's orders, as well as Rowan's sworn statement about the content of Mercer's unofficial note, and the reason why he had withheld it from Fox, would have cleared up some of the fog which still hangs over these early days of the war. Why did not Fox assert himself? Was he afraid, as he had stated in his letter to Blair, of injuring the government—meaning Seward and possibly Lincoln himself—by divulging how the *Powhatan* matter, and with it the entire Sumter affair, had been handled?

Lincoln now had done everything possible to avert an armed clash. He had kept Fox and his war fleet out of Charleston harbor; he had given Anderson a plain intimation to yield, had advised him of the proper date, had slipped information to the Confederates which would keep them quiescent until his surrender, and had taken steps to secure Fort Pickens ahead of the deadline. These preparations had been minutely co-ordinated so as to culminate at the same time. All the pieces on the political chessboard had been moved into position by a champion player.

The next move was up to Jefferson Davis. If he used sound judgment, and if everyone else did his part, the danger of war would be over by April 13. Lincoln spent the slow-moving hours in lonely anxiety. There was nothing for him to do but walk the floor and hope for the best. One may well believe his statement to Senator Orville Browning, made a few weeks later, that "all the troubles and anxieties of his life had not equalled those which [preceded] the fall of Sumter."[61] The issue between war and peace was quivering in a precarious balance.

As Lincoln reviewed the situation from every angle, it struck him that the Confederates might checkmate him by a simple countermove. They could offer to feed Anderson and his men on purely humanitarian grounds, thereby turning Fox's expedition into a mockery. Was not provisioning its avowed purpose? It would have been a joke in Lincoln's own style, and perhaps a good laugh was what the country needed to ease the tension. To those more seriously inclined the offer should have appealed as a generous gesture. Even Southern hotheads might have approved, if the act had been accompanied by a proclamation that the Confederate government, while not promising to sustain the Sumter garrison indefinitely, had no wish to see it starve in the midst of plenty.

In whatever way the fleet reacted to this stratagem, whether it departed or stayed outside the bar doing nothing, it would be made to look foolish; it no longer had any reason to enter the harbor, and if it did, it would be in the role of a transgressor. Anderson might have declined to accept food as a gift from the Charleston authorities, as he had done once before on the ground that army regulations compelled him to procure his supplies by contract; but if he again rejected the offer by such legalistic hairsplitting, he would forfeit the sympathy of the North. The President, however, soon dismissed these troublesome thoughts from his mind. Jefferson Davis was a slave to orthodoxy, and his sense of humor was stunted.

As Lincoln had foreseen, the crisis at Fort Sumter came to a head on April 11. On that day Anderson was asked to state definitely when he would abandon the work. The garrison had been on short rations for several days, and the men were so weakened that they could no longer perform fatiguing work. The officers were subsisting on a daily diet of two crackers and a tiny piece of pork.[62] Could Anderson do anything but give up? Or would he first want to see what the fleet did? And would the fleet carry out the negative role assigned to it?

Lincoln had cause to be worried. On April 5, prior to receiving the April 4 letter from the War Department, Anderson had written a report which reached Washington on the eighth. In it he had gone as far as he dared in criticizing his superiors. He had just been shown Crawford's telegram, as Lincoln had anticipated, and had been justly aroused by it. Was he really going to be starved into submission with the consent of his own government? He complained:

I cannot but think that Mr. Crawford misunderstood what he has heard . . . as I cannot think that the Gov-

ernment would abandon [my command] without instructions and without advice. . . . After thirty odd
years of service I do not wish it to be said that I have
treasonably abandoned a post . . . I am entitled to this
act of justice. . . .[63]

The intention to weaken Anderson's morale had
succeeded, but the result was not what Lincoln had
expected. A man who entertained such sentiments
would fight for his personal honor, if for nothing else,
unless he was ordered to do otherwise. Lincoln could
only trust that this faithful officer would correctly con-
strue the letter then on the way to him as a definite
order to surrender. For the rest, the President had to
rely on the behavior of the fleet.

On April 12, Anderson finally resolved his doubts.
He announced to the Southern emissaries that he
would evacuate the fort, but not until the fifteenth,
and then he added some ifs and ands which made his
proposition unacceptable. It was not Lincoln's fault
that Anderson could stretch the time of his resistance
three days beyond the anticipated limit. If Beauregard had stopped sending supplies to the fort during
the first week in April, its surrender by the twelfth
would have been inevitable. Beauregard never accounted for his fateful decision and, so far as is known,
was not taken to task for it.

Anderson was a brave and well-intentioned officer,
but the situation had become too complex for him. He
either failed to comprehend the meaning of what Lincoln had tried so hard to convey to him, or was not
sure enough to act on it. Subsequently he confided
to Fox that he felt hurt at what he thought was the

neglect of the government "in not informing him of
various matters,"[64] suggesting that the orders should
have been spelled out for him. Forced to assume a
responsibility beyond his station and capacity, he let
military tradition guide his actions, and military tradition demanded that he hold out to the last.

Two weeks later Lincoln was to write to him, ab-
solving him from any blame for not having been able
to decode Cameron's message:

A few days ago I caused an official letter to be
written to you through the War Department. . . . I
now write this, as a purely private and social letter,
to say I shall be much gratified to see you here at your
earliest convenience, when . . . I can personally testify
my appreciation of your services and fidelity; and,
perhaps, explain some things on my part, which you
may not have understood.[65]

No record has been found of Anderson's visit to the
White House. What it was that he had not understood
probably will remain forever unknown. All that can
be safely conjectured is that it was something the President did not care—or dare—to put into writing, not
even in a private letter.

Unfortunately, the Confederate authorities also
acted contrary to Lincoln's expectations. Now would
have been the time for them to deliberate coolly and
restrain their impetuosity. But at this momentous
hour, when the exercise of cool judgment was of the
greatest import, Jefferson Davis lost his head. For-

gotten were the newly installed searchlights, the
strengthened batteries, the odds against the supply
boats which would have been exposed to an encircling
fire, forgotten the missing pilots, the absence of buoys
and Anderson's oil shortage. All that Davis could
visualize was a "conflict with the guns of Fort Sumter
and the naval forces of the United States in combina-
tion."[66] But what looked like "the naval forces of the
United States" was in fact a weak fleet, intermingled
with unarmed merchant ships, which had been denied
entrance into the harbor, thus creating the illusion
of an invincible armada.[67] The President of the Confederacy succumbed to a nightmare which the light
of the coming day would have dissipated.

And so Davis ordered the bombardment. Anderson
withstood it for thirty-four hours, then marched out
with the Stars and Stripes flying, proud that he had
upheld the glory of the Army. The Northern public,
unaware that Anderson had bungled Lincoln's superb
peace effort, feted him as a national hero.

It was during the night of April 12 and 13, while
Fox was still anxiously awaiting the arrival of the *Powhatan*, that Fate, in a spirit of irony, furnished an anti-
climax to the drama in which it had played such a
treacherous role. While shells were hurled back and
forth across Charleston harbor, Federal troops reinforced Fort Pickens quietly, smoothly and without
bloodshed. Not until the next morning did the Confederates learn of the coup, and then took no hostile
action.

Almost all the President's calculations had worked
out to a nicety. If Scott had made Lincoln endorse the

order to Captain Adams, or had sent it by rail, if Beauregard had tightened his food blockade sooner, if Anderson had surrendered on the specified days, or if the Confederates had held their fire a few hours longer, there would have been no war. Such was the narrow margin by which Lincoln lost his greatest triumph, that of maintaining peace under most trying circumstances. Would he continue to keep the country out of war after this heartbreaking setback? The next days were to provide the answer.

4

Did It Have To Be War?

THE FIRST PHASE of the pending crisis was over. It had ended on an uncertain note. The fact that no man on either side had been killed or injured by enemy action inspired faith in both camps that a break still could be avoided. True, the American flag had been fired on, but that had happened before without leading to war. In January 1861 the *Star of the West* had been fired on when she entered Charleston Harbor in an endeavor to provision Fort Sumter but, due to the self-restraint of the Buchanan administration, the excitement had quickly subsided. Secretary of War Holt, whose loyalty to the Union was unquestioned, far from reprimanding Anderson, had commended him for not returning the fire of the South Carolina battery which had forced the relief ship to turn back. "You rightly designate the firing . . . as 'an act of war, . . .'" he declared. "As, however, it . . . was prompted by the passions of a highly inflamed population . . . your forbearance . . . is fully approved by the President."[1] There was hope that Lincoln would take the same calm view.

Buchanan had been in harmony with public opinion, for the *Star of the West* incident had left the North cold. One may read in *The Diary of a Public Man:*

I am [surprised] at the indifference, not to say apathy, with which this overt defiance to the Federal authority and this positive insult to the Federal flag have been received. . . . Certainly, since we are not at this moment in the blaze of civil war, there would seem to be little reason that we shall be overtaken by it at all.[2]

The logic of the Public Man was irrefutable, his forecast well founded. Now that the flag had again been fired on, the North was no more anxious to fight than it had been on the former occasion. Nicolay and Hay complained bitterly about the prevailing "perversion" of the public mind.[3] "The loyal states had suffered the siege of Sumter . . . with . . . indifference," they wrote.[4] They analyzed the prevailing sentiment and found it wanting:

The desire for peace; the hope of compromise; the persistent disbelief in the extreme purposes of the South; and, strangest of all, a certain national lethargy, utterly impossible to account for—all seemed to mark a decadence of patriotic feeling. . . .[5]

James G. Blaine, a leading Republican, years afterward offered a simple explanation for what the two secretaries had found unaccountable. "The overwhelming public desire after all," he said, "was for peace, and the overwhelming public opinion was against the extremists who would, by any possibility, precipitate war."[6]

Peace then was admittedly the wish of the majority. Would Lincoln, like Buchanan, attune himself to it and continue his conciliatory policy? His public record was reassuring. He had always talked peace. Only recently, in his Inaugural, he had deprecated a resort to arms. "Suppose you go to war," he had counseled, "you cannot fight always; and when, after much loss on both sides, . . . you cease fighting, the identical old questions . . . are again upon you."[7] A sensible statement, with which it was difficult to disagree. Lincoln had also promised that he would do his duty, "unless [his] rightful masters, the American people, shall withhold the requisite means, or, in some authoritative manner, direct the contrary."[8] If this meant anything, it meant that he would not, in fact could not, constitutionally make war without the consent of Congress, and Congress was not in session. As a Congressman, Lincoln had endorsed an amendment to a resolution which declared that the Mexican war had been "unnecessarily and unconstitutionally commenced by the President."[9] And the secretary of the Peace Conference had recorded a statement of Lincoln's which inspired additional faith: "If I shall ever come to the great office of the President, . . . I shall take an oath. I shall swear that I will . . . to the best of my ability preserve, protect and defend the Constitution of the United States. This is a great and solemn duty."[10] L. E. Chittenden, one of Lincoln's ardent admirers, remembered that the President-elect had added this significant afterthought: "It is not the Constitution as I would like to have it, but as it *is*, that is to be defended."[11] Lincoln might even call for a plebiscite. Crittenden had proposed one when his compromise had been under discussion in January, and Stephen Douglas had supported it. "Why not allow the people to pass on these questions?" the Senator from Illinois had queried.[12] Greeley of the *New York Tribune* thought that if the compromise had been submitted to the voters, a majority would have ratified it.[13] But in making this proposal the two Senators were far ahead of their time—and ours.

On April 13 a delegation from the Virginia Convention called at the White House to inquire what the President's intentions were. His reply, read from a written memorandum, was evasive and ambiguous. Nevertheless, the delegation left in the belief that he had "expressly disclaimed all purpose of war."[14]

Lincoln, however, contemplated no immediate session of Congress, nor was he considering a plebiscite. While the guns were still thundering in Charleston Harbor, he had made his decision, and it was entirely his own. At this fateful moment he did not even call a Cabinet meeting. The members did meet, but "as by a common impulse,"[15] so Nicolay and Hay reported.

They deliberated among themselves, briefly, informally and aimlessly; for while they talked, Lincoln in the solitude of his office was shaping the destiny of thirty-odd million people.

The unbelievable was happening. One man was taking it on himself to determine the fate of the nation. Still more incredible, it was the same man who, in 1848, had written to his partner Herndon:

Kings had always been involving . . . their people in wars. . . . This, our convention understood to be the most oppressive of all kingly oppressions; and they resolved to so frame the Constitution that no one man should hold the power of bringing this oppression upon us.[16]

"No one man." Yet when the Cabinet members at last were invited to meet with the President, their opinions were not even asked for. All they did was listen to the President's announcement that he had prepared a call for 75,000 militia. They concurred with a docility which did them no honor. Nicolay and Hay were more than docile; they heartily approved this manifestation of a one-man government. "The time had come," they wrote piously, "when . . . his judgment alone must guide, his sole will determine. . . ."[17] Was this democracy?

Curiously, it was Blair, the most belligerent of Lincoln's advisers, who later ventured a covert disapproval. "It was assuming the greatest responsibility ever assumed by any man," he said; but he waited twenty-one years before he made this quasi-critical comment.[18]

In spite of the call for troops, war was not a foregone conclusion. Everything depended on the use to which the troops would be put. If they were going to be employed for defensive purposes only, no one would object, probably not even the Confederates. The border states would have no reason to join the Confederacy; they were for the Union but they were against coercion. The wording of the call therefore would be all decisive.

On April 14 a ray of sunshine broke through the gathering clouds. The *Washington Sunday Morning Chronicle* carried this short telegraphic item:

Pensacola, April 13—Fort Pickens was reinforced last night.

The editor of the *Chronicle* evidently did not realize the importance of this short telegram, for he printed it on the second page.[19] But to Lincoln it carried a message pregnant with meaning. He now knew definitely that the Gulf fort was safe and that the loss of Fort Sumter would not be too bitterly resented. Except for the bloodless bombardment, his plan had worked out in complete conformity with his hopes and wishes. The proclamation had not yet been issued and, if already sent to the press, could be recalled. Most observers, if cognizant of all facts, would have rejoiced that the threat of an armed conflict had vanished.

On the next day, April 15, the proclamation was made public. Universally interpreted as an open declaration of war, it rocked the country to its foundations. The troops were to deal with "combinations too powerful to be suppressed by the ordinary course of judicial proceedings," and "probably" would be used first to repossess the forts and other property which had been taken over by the seceded states. Moreover, it commanded "the persons composing the combinations aforesaid" to retire peacefully to their respective abodes within twenty days.[20] The proclamation must have come as a surprise even to the American minister at London, to whom Seward had written a bare five days before that "Only an imperial and despotic government could subjugate thoroughly disaffected and insurrectionary members of the State."[21] Nevertheless, what Seward had declared impossible, except at the hands of an imperial and despotic government, had come to pass.

It is strange that so few critics have discussed the pros and cons of whether war was the inevitable, or even the logical consequence of the shooting at Charleston. With almost complete unanimity they have subscribed to the misconception that it was. Yet, to arrive at this conclusion one must ignore the fact that the President, heedless of his recent assurances, had given the electorate neither an opportunity to "withhold the requisite means," nor one "to direct the contrary." One must ignore the ease with which Buchanan had peaceably disposed of the *Star of the West* case. Furthermore, one must ignore the lesson of history that in a national crisis the ruler of a country has it within his power either to harness or inflame the popular mind. Lincoln's wise Attorney General expressed it tersely: *"Public opinion,"* he confided to his diary, "is never spontaneous. . . . It is always a manufactured article. . . . Bold and active rulers *make* it on their side."[22] The much abused Buchanan had demonstrated the truth of this epigram by refusing to become unduly excited; and within the year, following the *Trent* affair, the Queen's consort Albert was to quench England's clamor for war with a few soothing words. Lincoln would have had an easier task than the prince consort had, because the majority of the Northern people were clamoring for peace, not for war.

Not everyone who stood in the forefront of contemporary events took as catastrophic a view of the Sumter episode as Lincoln did. Jefferson Davis thought that "separation is not yet of necessity final— there has been no blood spilled. . . ."[23] In Washington, Secretary Welles put his opinion into very similar words. "Until blood was spilled," he wrote later, "there was hope of conciliation."[24] Significantly, these two statesmen not only denied that the incident need lead to war, but they were also discussing an early reestablishment of the Union.

The highly respected former Senator Howell Cobb of Georgia, who had been elected president of the Confederate Provisional Congress, saw only continued peace in the offing and told the people of the South that "they could go on cultivating their crops."[25] Governor John Letcher of Virginia shared Cobb's belief that the affair in Charleston Harbor would not involve the country in civil war. Ten days after Anderson's surrender Letcher issued a proclamation advising the people to gather "not in the military service of the State," but "to return to their usual avocations, in connection with the trade and commerce of the country."[26] James Guthrie of Kentucky, a strong Unionist who once had served in Pierce's Cabinet and had been seriously considered by Lincoln for a like post, probably reflected the grim humor of the man on the street, when he said, ". . . [we] are now going to cut each other's throats; and why? Because Presidents Lincoln and Davis couldn't settle the etiquette upon which the troops were to be withdrawn from Fort Sumter."[27]

Conservatives throughout the nation saw no cause for a clash of arms. They held that the Charleston gun duel had been an isolated melee, and, both sides having preserved their prestige, the chapter was closed. The Federal government had secured Fort Pickens and thereby maintained its national authority. It could rest on its laurels. The South could boast of having taken Sumter; to extend the fighting by attacking the North would border on insanity. Out of a total of some 31,000,000 people, only five million lived in the cotton states, and nearly half of these were slaves. Moreover, the border states provided a buffer which made a physical contact of the two sections difficult. Southern fire-eaters might shout that one of them could lick six Yankees, or that they would be in Faneuil Hall by May, but those who bore the responsibility knew better. Even after four more states had joined the Confederacy, it lacked everything for a war of aggression—the motive, the will and the strength. Jefferson Davis expressed the attitude of the Confed-

eracy concisely in an address to his Congress on April
29. "We protest solemnly in the face of mankind," he
averred, "that we desire peace at any sacrifice save
that of honor . . . we seek no conquest, no aggrandize-
ment, no cession of any kind. . . . All we want is to be
let alone."[28] The realism of this declaration precluded
any doubts as to its sincerity. But perhaps the most
convincing proof that the South did not consider herself at war with her northern neighbor was that Anderson and his men had not been made prisoners, had in
fact been allowed to depart in honor with their flags
flying and their drums beating the national air.[29]

The reason the inevitability of the Civil War has
rarely been questioned may be that most histories of
this period have been written by Northern sympathizers who hesitated to admit that any of Lincoln's acts
could have been unwise or contrary to democratic
principles. A modern scholar who had the courage
to voice his misgivings did so cautiously: "Must the
Sumter incident become the appeal to arms? . . .
Did it have to be war?" he asked. But he left the twin
questions hanging in mid-air.[30] Yet, had he answered
them, he would have been more closely in harmony
with the spirit of Lincoln himself. Senator Trumbull
pointed out to Congress:

I know enough of honest Abraham Lincoln to know
that he will not regard as his truest friends men who
. . . swear that everything he does is right. He . . . is
honest enough, and great enough, . . . to know that
he is not perfect . . . that some measures that he has
adopted may not be the wisest. He will think better

of a man who has the candor to [suggest this], than he will of the sycophant who tells him, "all is right that you do, and you cannot do wrong. . . ."[31]

Right or wrong, it may be accepted as a fact that Lincoln honestly believed the war to be necessary, or at least expedient, for he would not have started it on any other conceivable grounds. The question naturally arises what prompted his decision. Welles was one of the few who attempted to supply a clue. He recorded that in March 1861 "the elder Blair [had] sought an interview with the President, to whom he entered his protest against non-action. . . . His earnestness and indignation aroused and electrified the President. . . ."[32] Welles was a keen observer, and if he saw a change in Lincoln's attitude after this interview, he probably was right. But what may have impressed the President more than a mere protest against inaction was Blair's assurance that the war would end speedily and victoriously.

Lincoln's sudden turnabout was ascribed in other quarters either to a feeling of relief on his part that the decision had been made for him, or to one of frustration that things had slipped out of his hands. Patient men, they said, whose endurance has been strained beyond the breaking point, are apt to swing from one extreme to the other; and Lincoln was a very patient man. Had he not given indication of his suppressed anger when in his proclamation he had referred to "wrongs already long enough endured?"

Nevertheless, neither of these suggestions carries conviction. Lincoln scarcely would have felt relief at

a decision which ran counter to his aims and wishes;
and if he threw the whole nation into the abyss of war
while in a fit of temper, he stepped completely out of
character. There is no other case on record where he
made an important decision during an outburst of pas-
sion or petulance.

Southerners had their own ideas on the subject.
They accused Lincoln of having maneuvered for war
all along, and of having tricked them into becoming the
attackers. E. A. Pollard, wartime editor of the *Richmond Examiner*, had this to say: "The point with the
[Federal] government was to devise some artifice for
the relief of Fort Sumter . . . which would have the
effect of inaugurating the war . . . under a plausible
and convenient pretence."[33] Jefferson Davis argued
in the same vein, and still was resentful twenty years
later at the way he thought Lincoln had victimized
him. "The attempt to represent us as the *aggressors,*"
he wrote, ". . . is as unfounded as the complaint made
by the wolf against the lamb. . . . He who makes the
assault is not necessarily . . . he that . . . fires the first
gun." When one is threatened with a deadly weapon,
he elucidated, one would be a fool to wait before
striking down his arms until he made good his threat.[34]

Robert Tomes, although Northern in sentiment, was
inclined to support this interpretation. While also considering other possibilities, he believed the Union fleet
at Charleston may have served the purpose of goading
the citizens of Charleston "into the first act of hostil-
ity, while the Government was performing an obvious
act of duty in making an attempt to supply a starving
garrison with provisions."[35]

In 1881 Nicolay, Lincoln's senior secretary, also came surprisingly close to adopting the Southern point of view. In *The Outbreak of the Rebellion* he noted that on the first of April, 1861, Seward's conciliatory policy "gave way before the President's . . . carefully matured purpose to force rebellion to put itself flagrantly . . . in the wrong by attacking Fort Sumter."[36] A few years afterward, when Nicolay and Hay became partners in compiling Lincoln's life story, they suggested an additional motive. "Whether the expedition [to Fort Sumter] would fail or succeed," they wrote, "was . . . of minor importance. . . . He [Lincoln] was looking through Sumter . . . beyond the insulted flag to the avenging nation."[37] The logic of this statement clearly is faulty. Nothing but failure of the expedition, with an attendant Confederate attack, could have stirred the North into avenging action. Success, peaceably achieved, would have left nothing to avenge. Only by presuming that Lincoln had been counting on failure could the authors make out a case at all, and even then their opinion should be taken with a grain of salt, because in those early days they had not enjoyed the President's confidence enough to reflect his real thoughts. However, when the two secretaries worked on his biography many years later, they had access to his correspondence, including the warlike messages he had sent to General Scott, Alexander Stephens and others in the winter of 1860-1861. Written during the months preceding his arrival in Washington, the letters show that Lincoln had then been determined to assert the authority of government, even to go to war for it if necessary. Taken by themselves, they tend to bear out Nicolay's and Hay's conclusion, but their separation from other and contradictory factors distorts the picture.

Anti-administration politicians advanced still another theory. They charged the President with having started the war in order to save his party. In 1861 the Republicans were a patchwork of factions which had little in common with one another. Recent local elections had gone against them, and the change in public sentiment foreshadowed a possible disintegration of their organization. War would not only close their ranks but also would silence the opposition. In other words, these critics imputed to Lincoln motives of a partisan nature, although not necessarily partisan in the narrow sense of the word. What he may have feared, if the Democrats came into power, was that they might agree to a partition of the United States, and this he was determined to prevent at any cost. The weakness of this theory is that the Democrats also were split into peace and war factions, hence it is hard to tell what they would have done if they had been held responsible for the results.

To ascertain Lincoln's true motives is a task most chroniclers have shied away from, perhaps because it calls for answers to some delicate questions which they have been loath to explore:

What prompted Lincoln to declare war on the South?

If he did think war unavoidable, why did he wait six weeks before striking?

Having waited that long, why did he indulge in such desperate haste?

Why did he assume sole responsibility for a proclamation which was sure to have far-reaching consequences?

In view of the critical situation, why did he not hurry Congress into session?

How can his pacific utterances be reconciled with his belligerent ones and, moreover, with his belligerent action?

On the face of it, Lincoln's war declaration is totally incomprehensible. Only a short time before he had scorned war with his common-sense observation that, after great losses on both sides, the old questions still would remain. This reasoning was as sound on April 15 as it had been on the day on which he had promulgated it. Why then did he refute his own argument, the most powerful ever advanced against the carnage of war?

The second query is as puzzling as the first. If Lincoln wanted to use force, why had he not prepared for it from the very beginning? Yet during the first weeks in office Lincoln had done nothing to arouse the people; on the contrary, he had enjoined his Cabinet from antagonizing the Secessionists by either speech or deeds.[38] For some reason the fighting spirit, so plainly apparent in his letters to Scott and others, seemed to have gone out of him. All he had done was to order the reinforcement of Fort Pickens, but this could scarcely be called aggression, since the work had never been out of Federal possession.

The third and fourth riddles are posed by the abruptness of Lincoln's conversion from an advocate of peace to one of war, and by a haste so precipitate

that he did not even seek the views of his official advisers, his personal friends or the members of Congress. Yet only a short time before he had earnestly
pleaded that nothing valuable could be lost by taking
time, and that no good object could be frustrated by it.

The final enigma, the incompatibility of his bellicose
acts with his pacific pronouncements as well as with
his action, seems equally inexplicable. Nevertheless, a
key to it must exist, as one must for the other incongruities. But this key must open all the locked doors,
not just one, because these problems are interde-
pendent and inseparable.

As is usually the case with deep and independent
thinkers, Lincoln's ideas were not cast in a rigid mold.
Rather they changed with changing conditions. In
the months preceding the fall of Sumter he vacillated
frequently and rapidly, in conformity with political
developments. Immediately after his election, when
Southern disaffection was still largely a matter of oratory, it was natural for him to let matters take their
course and follow a "programme of 'masterly inactivity.'" A few weeks later South Carolina seceded;
thereupon he resolved to "put the foot down firmly,"
even to the extent of repossessing lost Federal properties. But as his inauguration approached, this resolution flagged. Why?

From all appearances this reversion was due to the
soothing influence of Seward, who was convinced that
war could be avoided by a swap of Fort Sumter for
a more secure Fort Pickens. Yet this contemplated
coup itself presents a paradox. Inasmuch as Lincoln

was firmly determined to resist a partition of the country, how could he assent to a step which was the very negation of this dogma?

Most likely it was Seward again who overcame this obstacle. Through clever and not unsound reasoning he managed to harmonize the two conflicting principles, by predicting that time would lead to a lasting reconciliation, and that the time would not be long. In this forecast he was not alone, for many prominent men on both sides shared this opinion.[39] John H. Reagan of Texas, later Postmaster General in Jefferson Davis' Cabinet, had gone so far as to predict that the South, if left alone, would voluntarily come back into the Union after one season.[40] Even Chase, the austere Secretary of the Treasury, had been willing to let the Secessionists try the experiment of separation because he felt confident of their early return.[41] This prospect was further sustained by news from the South. Dissatisfaction there already was spreading at a rapid pace. The western states of the Confederacy, deprived of protection by the Federal army, were demanding troops, who were not available. Eastern Confederate leaders were complaining for various selfish reasons, such as that the political plums had not been distributed equitably. Ironically, the citizens of Charleston were the most disillusioned. They had expected to profit from the resumption of the slave trade, and had shouldered a heavy tax load in anticipation of it, only to see the enactment of a Constitution containing a clause against importation of slaves. Resentment ran so high that some South Carolinians were openly discussing the advisability of seceding from the Confed-

eracy and placing themselves under a British protec-
torate.[42]

In view of these circumstances, Seward was justified
in his belief that the disunited states might soon become united again, and that Fort Sumter could temporarily be yielded without abandoning Lincoln's
guiding principle.

The President's message to Congress May 26, 1862,
lends support to this assumption. "The insurgents,"
he declared, "committed the flagrant act of civil war
by the bombardment and capture of Fort Sumter,
which cut off the hope of immediate conciliation."[43]
These words furnish undeniable proof that prior
to the attack on Anderson Lincoln not only had regarded conciliation as feasible, but had hoped for it.

The calming influence which Seward exerted on
the President had begun to manifest itself soon after
his appointment as Secretary of State, as shown by the
alterations he caused to be made in the forthcoming
Inaugural. It had been composed and printed in
Springfield, and Lincoln had asked his entourage for
comments. Originally the President-elect had proposed to say that "all the power at my disposal will be
used to reclaim the public property and places which
have fallen." His friend Browning suggested he delete
this threat, but it was Seward who definitely wooed
the President-elect away from it, urging him to say that
"the power confided to me shall be used . . . with discretion . . . according to . . . circumstances . . . and with
a view and a hope of a peaceful solution. . . ."[44] Lincoln would not bend that far, but he did soften his
language appreciably. In his new version he promised

"to hold, occupy and possess the property and places belonging to the Government." With the barrier of forcible reclamation removed, the door to peace was left open.

Lincoln would not have rewritten his draft if he had not thought Seward's plan of giving up Sumter for Pickens looked promising. Once having sanctioned it, he gave his Secretary of State full authority to carry it out. Seward cheerfully took advantage of this privilege. He usurped the functions of the War and Navy Departments, delegated his power to subaltern officers, and played fast and loose with military procedures. Convinced that his scheme would succeed, he gave the Southern Commissioners sanguine promises and looked with buoyancy toward a happy conclusion. So did Lincoln. The reinforcement of Fort Pickens, he said a few weeks later, would have better enabled the country "to accept the evacuation of Fort Sumter as a military *necessity.*"[45]

Then things began to go awry. A storm delayed the delivery of a vital order, a self-important general let it go out without a proper endorsement, a conscientious navy officer refused to obey it. Lincoln's confidence in his chief adviser went into a decline, and the "Thoughts for the President's Consideration" which Seward sent to Lincoln on April 1 undoubtedly contributed to his diminishing influence. His proposal to make war on England, France or Spain, in order to bring the North and South into a common front, must have frightened the President. Nevertheless, inasmuch as he had approved Seward's plan, he continued to back it, and did so loyally until it collapsed.

This premise appears to account for the contradictions between Lincoln's peaceful and warlike utterances. The quick changes in the situation were reflected by concurrent fluctuations in his thinking.
Hardly had words been spoken or letters written when
their underlying ideas had to be gainsaid because they
no longer represented either the altered situation or
his latest views.

Lincoln was not alone in finding it difficult to adjust
himself to the constantly recurring shifts in the political currents. Governor Letcher of Virginia noted in
a proclamation on November 15, 1860:

Events crowd . . . each other with astounding rapidity.
The scenes of to-day are dissolved by the developments of to-morrow. The opinions now entertained
may be totally revolutionized by unforeseen and unan-
ticipated occurrences that an hour or a day may bring
forth.[46]

Lincoln's judgment doubtless was swayed by the
same unpredictable squalls; but valid as this explanation may be in regard to his frequent change of views,
it does not account for his hurry in resorting to armed
force, for delaying the convening of Congress and for
assuming the sole responsibility of taking the last fateful step. Here again conjecture must largely replace
factual evidence, of which unfortunately there is but
little.

When Lincoln allowed himself to be diverted from
his first aim, to repossess the lost forts, he probably
did so with the understanding that he would return to

it should the Sumter-Pickens plan come to nothing. This now had happened; but some precious weeks had already been lost, and if there was to be war, he had to act promptly, while popular excitement was at its height. If he gave the people time for a sobering second thought, he might not be able to gain their support. There must be no hesitancy, not even a discussion with his Cabinet, which so far had never agreed on any important issue, and where Seward might offer stubborn and eloquent opposition. To call an early meeting of Congress likewise was not politic, for its deliberations would go on endlessly and kill the war spirit before it had reached the ignition point. Fortunately, a catch phrase was temptingly at hand: "The flag has been insulted." Admittedly, it was an apppeal to emotion rather than to judgment but, if quickly applied, it would do its work. It had never failed before, it would not fail now.

With his uncanny skill in reading the public mind, Lincoln had correctly appraised its volatility. Like a powerful intoxicant, his proclamation turned apathetic, peace-loving citizens into an unreasoning mob in a matter of hours. Parades stamped through the streets, orators delivered superheated speeches. Men expressing misgivings were at the mercy of mass hysteria, and found their refuge in silence. "There is no tyranny so despotic," wrote a contemporary, "as that of public opinion among a free people."[47] The President's secretaries were jubilant:

The lion of the North was fully roused. . . . War sermons from pulpits; war speeches in every assemblage;

tenders of troops; offers of money; . . . every city ra-
diant with bunting; every village-green a mustering
ground. . . . The very children abandoned their old-
time school-games and played . . . soldiering.[48]

No one recognized that the excitement was a straw fire
which, fed only with seductive phrases, was bound
to consume itself shortly. No one foresaw that within
a year voluntary enlistment would have stopped completely; that martial music would have given way to
dirges, and that instead of reading fiery proclamations
the people would be anxiously scanning casualty lists.
    But all this was still below the horizon. For the pres-
ent the outlook was bright, and everyone felt sure of
an early victory.

    Still unanswered is the question of why Lincoln con-
sidered war the only way, or even the best way, to end
the crisis. It is the most important of all questions,
and also the hardest to answer. What thoughts coursed
through the President's mind while he pondered his
decision will never be known. He did not want war,
nor had he unconditionally committed himself to it,
as demonstrated by his willingness to evacuate Fort
Sumter; nevertheless, he had made his position regarding secession very clear: his convictions bound him
firmly to the preservation of the Union. To a delegate
of the Peace Convention he had said, "In a choice of
evils, war may not always be the worst."[49] The choice
of evils was now upon him. He realized that war was
an evil; doubtlessly he also envisioned the eventual
extinction of slavery, which would settle the sectional

friction without the outpouring of blood. The growing unrest in the seceded states, indicating their early return, also weighed heavily in favor of peace. Unhappily the extinction of slavery was still far off, and while the cotton states might be dissatisfied, pride and the reluctance of politicians to step down would act as deterrents to immediate conciliation, or might prevent it altogether. Furthermore, if the Confederacy were tolerated a few months longer, the use of force would no longer appeal to the people of the North. One does not slap a man's face for an insult suffered several months before, and another opportunity like the Sumter affair was not likely to recur.

So far the arguments for and against the two divergent paths were about evenly balanced. The decisive factor would be the probable length of the conflict, if conflict it was to be. A long war would bring the nation to the verge of bankruptcy, both materially and morally, and would leave behind wounds which might not heal for decades. Even an unbroken Union was not worth such a terrifying price. A short war, on the other hand, might be more beneficial than harmful. At a small expenditure of human lives it would reunite the country, and serve as a hands-off warning to European rulers who hovered like vultures over Mexico and some Atlantic islands.

The core of the problem therefore, as it must have appeared to Lincoln, was how long it would take to subdue the South. Not very long, he thought. Preponderance in man power, in industrial capacity, in monetary resources and easy access to foreign supplies were on his side. Besides, the North had a small but well-trained army of regulars, against whom amateur soldiers would be no match.

We have it from Lincoln's own lips that the question of how long the war would last was pressing on his mind. A few days after his call to arms he conferred with Carl Schurz, whom he had recently appointed minister to Spain, but who had volunteered to postpone his departure in order to raise a few German cavalry regiments. Lincoln dissuaded his visitor. The war, he remarked, might be over soon, although he was not so sanguine in this respect as others whose opinions he valued. Seward, for instance, "was speaking of sixty or ninety days." Schurz then called on General Scott, who told him that "if there was to be war at all, it would be short, and over long before any cavalry volunteers could be fitted for active service."[50] How many other prominent men the President consulted is not known but, regardless of their number, their stature demonstrates that he had tried earnestly to estimate the duration of the coming conflict.

One man who may have strongly influenced Lincoln's thinking was the elder Blair, who believed that the war would not last long and that it was preferable to an uneasy peace. His son Montgomery, who usually mirrored the opinions of his father, had expressed them in a letter to Fox a few weeks before. He had written on January 31, 1861:

I do not at all believe . . . that the application of force . . . will so exasperate the Sections as to render reconciliation impossible . . . the real good feeling which the people of the North have for the South will work off all bitterness in a short time . . . and with less of blood and treasure than any alarmist will believe. . . .[51]

Lincoln placed great faith in the political wisdom of the Blair family, and one of his remarks to Browning, made a month later, was almost an exact echo of Montgomery Blair's letter. Lincoln, so Browning reported in his diary on February 9, "agreed with me that far less evil and bloodshed would result from an effort to maintain the Union and the Constitution, than from disruption and the formation of two confederacies."[52] This remark indicates that before Lincoln had come under Seward's influence, he was willing to wage a short war rather than one of much greater magnitude which, he feared, would have to be fought later.

That Lincoln did not anticipate a long war is further attested by the small number of troops he called out, and by his limiting their time of service to ninety days. True, these limitations were imposed on him by the Constitution, but he already had slid around its edges in issuing his call and was to ride roughshod over it in the weeks to come.

Above all, however, Lincoln's faith in a short war may have rested on his reckoning that the strong Unionist sentiment in the border states would keep them from seceding. If so, the resistance of the Confederacy would soon be overcome. After everything was said and done, it was the attitude of the border states, more than any other factor, which would deter-

mine the length of the conflict. Douglas, whose political acumen was second to none, had predicted as far
back as New Year's Day, 1861, that if the border states
seceded, the war would be the most fearful the world
had ever seen and would go on for years.[53] Conversely,
if those states remained under the old flag, the war
would be speedily ended.

Recent indications of public opinion justified
Lincoln's optimism. Early in February immediate
secession had been decisively turned down by the
Virginia Convention, 122 to 30, and the electorate had
endorsed this vote, 100,536 to 45,161. Moreover, it
had added the provision that secession should first be
ratified by popular vote.[54] In Tennessee, 91,803
Unionists had stood firm against 24,749 Secessionists,
and the convention was not allowed to meet. The
Unionists had won 39 to 35 in the Arkansas convention, and in Missouri by the one-sided vote of 89 to 1.
North Carolina had elected 50 unconditional and 28
conditional Unionists against only 42 Secessionist delegates, and then had voted 47,323 to 46,672 that the
convention should not meet. Maryland, Delaware and
Kentucky had refused even to call a convention.[55]

In these circumstances it was small wonder that
Lincoln looked into the future through rose-colored
glasses. He had not forgotten Baldwin's prediction
that his state would go out if a shot were fired in
Charleston Harbor, but considering the overwhelming
Union sentiment in the border states, it appeared
doubtful that Virginia, even should she secede, would
be able to lead other states into the Confederacy. In

the President's judgment the cold figures of votes out-weighed the Virginian's gloomy forecast.

Lincoln's apparently inconsistent and contradictory actions during the first weeks of his incumbency may therefore be summarized as follows:

He decided on war, because he felt confident that it would be short, hence less costly in blood and treas-ure than the formation of two confederacies.

He waited six weeks before striking, because he hoped to forestall hostilities by an honorable surrender of Fort Sumter and a simultaneous strengthening of Fort Pickens.

He acted in haste, because the bombardment at Charleston furnished the impulse he needed to arouse an apathetic public. Delay might dampen the preva-lent war fever to the point of extinction.

He assumed sole responsibility for his proclamation, because he expected to meet opposition in his Cabinet. For a like reason he refrained from calling Congress into early session.

The contradictions betweeen his peaceful and war-like utterances were due to periodic changes in the situation, causing corresponding changes in his think-ing. There were five such well-defined periods. Prior to Lincoln's nomination he held war to be inevitable, but immediately after his election he decided to re-main inactive. When South Carolina seceded he once more became war-minded. A conciliatory period began when he fell under Seward's influence, and lasted until the surrender of Fort Sumter, after which he again reverted to belligerency. With events shaping his thinking during these five periods, the contradictions in his pronouncements appear logical rather than conflicting.

The press of the North agreed with Lincoln's belief in a short war and proclaimed it in extravagant terms.

"The nations of Europe," wrote the *New York Tribune* inelegantly, "may rest assured that Jeff. Davis & Co. will be swinging from the battlements at Washington . . . by the 4th of July. We spit upon a later and longer deferred justice."

Said the *New York Times:* "Let us make quick work. . . . A strong active 'pull together' will do our work . . . in thirty days."

The *Philadelphia Press* thought that "no man of sense would, for a moment, doubt that this much-ado-about-nothing could end in a month."

The *Cincinnati Commercial* was only slightly more conservative. It predicted that "the rebellion will be crushed out before the assemblage of Congress—no doubt of it."

The *Chicago Tribune* was equally confident. "Let the East get out of the way," it challenged. ". . . We can fight the battle, and successfully, within two or three months at the furthest. Illinois can whip the South by herself."[56]

The unanimous opinion of the Northern papers doubtless was encouraging to Lincoln, but in the end the course of future events depended to a fateful degree on the soundness or fallacy of his own judgment.

5

The Sumter Enigma

As THE MONTHS rolled by, the Sumter affair disappeared from the front pages of the newspapers, but it did not recede from the memory of the public. The gaps and incongruities in the official reports aroused a well-founded suspicion that important information had been withheld, and suspicion became tinged with resentment, when it became known that all chief participants had received substantial promotions despite their negative achievements.

Meigs, who as a captain in April 1861 had conspired with Captain Mercer and Lieutenant Porter to wreck Fox's expedition, was appointed colonel on May 14. The very next day he was made brigadier and quartermaster general,[1] in which capacity, by the way, he did excellent service. The elderly Mercer remained a captain, but before the year ended he was appointed to the Navy Retiring Board.[2] Porter was elevated to the rank of vice-admiral; and Captain Rowan, who had

withheld Mercer's personal note from Fox, was given
a newly built battleship, commanded the South Atlantic blockade squadron in 1864 and, after the war, became a rear admiral.[3] Fox, who had made himself
liable to court-martial by disobeying Cameron's orders
to enter Charleston Harbor regardless of possible resistance, was removed from the jurisdiction of the War
Department and given a high post in the Navy. Not a
single actor in the Sumter drama had been asked to
account for his conduct. It was natural that ugly
gossip spread and found a ready audience. Some
of this tongue-wagging may have come to Lincoln's
ears, but he had to maintain silence. Even his most
loyal followers could not be allowed to learn of his
machinations to force Anderson into surrender, and
the Northern governors, who were furnishing the
man power, must never doubt that the expedition had
been anything but what it had purported to be. For
the time being, the opening chapter of the war had to
stay wrapped in secrecy.

In spite of all efforts, however, part of the truth did
become known. The story of the clandestine messages
which Harvey had sent to Charleston, and which had
so mystified Welles, leaked out and unleashed a storm
in Congressional circles. Although Harvey had been
tucked away in far-off Lisbon, he soon found himself the target of violent attacks, which caused the
government considerable embarrassment. On July 13,
Senator Browning wrote in his diary that in caucus
Sumner had read aloud Harvey's dispatches, "giving
intelligence of what was going on in Washington." A
committee was appointed to call on the President and

demand the recall of the miscreant.[4] Seward tried to persuade the committee that it was sniffing at a false trail, but he was at a loss for a suitable explanation. Harvey, he declared awkwardly, being a correspondent and a favorite with some "old Whig" newspapers, had been imprudently entrusted with a state secret, and had blundered. "I thought it wrong," Seward added needlessly, "to punish a man for his stupid folly, when really he had committed no crime."[5] But what he failed to make clear was why a man who had committed a stupid folly and could not keep a state secret had been rewarded with—of all things—a diplomatic post.

As could be expected, the Congressmen were not impressed and continued to demand disciplinary action. Harvey showed himself a poor diplomat by writing naïve letters to the State Department, blabbing that he had only done as he was told. He thereby enlightened posterity, but not the members of the committee, who were not given access to this correspondence. They insisted on an answer to their question. Seward dillydallied until eventually the commotion died down, to Lincoln's intense relief. But inside Lincoln's own Cabinet suspicion lingered. Four years later Welles still nursed a grievance. He recorded in his diary that "it was Seward, Blair says, who informed Harvey and had him telegraph to Charleston. . . . This betrayal . . . did not interfere with his mission to Lisbon."[6] The strait-laced Welles could not conceive that it was this very "betrayal" which had led to Harvey's appointment in the first place.

Although Seward had quieted the curious-minded temporarily, the belief persisted many vital facts had been purposely hidden from view. Surprisingly, it was Fox who was the first to lift a corner of the protecting curtain. Anti-administration politicians kept scoffing at his effort to provision Fort Sumter, and their insinuations finally wore him down. On February 24, 1865, he submitted a report to the Secretary of the Navy, and in it he promised to give a full account of his role in the imbroglio.[7]

"The expedition," he began, ". . . has been referred to in the hope of throwing ridicule upon it and upon me. It is incomprehensible . . . that . . . any plan could provoke a sneer; nor does the shaft strike me. It falls upon the President, under whose sanction I acted." What the report was going to reveal, he continued, would "serve as materials for the vindication of the President." Fox then made an odd allusion to what he called "the secret history of this period."[8] The critics waxed triumphant. So there *was* a secret history, as they had been claiming all along. Fox's further statements funneled additional grist into their mill for, while ostensibly championing Lincoln's cause, he sounded as if he were attempting to clear his own record at the expense of the President's. He now disclosed for the first time two important communications between Lincoln and himself, one oral, the other in writing. The first dealt with his protest that the time allowed him for preparing the expedition was too short, a protest answered by an order to go ahead anyway;[9] in the second he had complained that, by having been deprived of the *Powhatan,* he had been robbed of all chances for success. Lincoln acknowledged both communications in a letter dated May 1, 1861, which Fox made public by attaching it to his report. It read in part:

Washington, D. C.
May 1, 1861

My dear Sir:

I sincerely regret that the failure of the late attempt to provision Fort Sumter should be the source of any annoyance to you . . . by an accident, for which you were in no wise responsible, and possibly I to some extent was, you were deprived of a war vessel, . . . which you deemed of great importance to the enterprize. . . .

You and I both anticipated that the cause of the country would be advanced by making the attempt to provision Fort Sumter, even if it should fail; and it is no small consolation now to feel that our anticipation is justified by the result.

Very truly your friend,
A. Lincoln[10]

This note must have been an eye-opener for Fox. A month before he had written to Blair: "I feel like abandoning my country, moving off somewhere. I am sick down to my heel";[11] and after the fiasco of his expedition he felt still more outraged. But the letter should have brought about a change in his feelings, what with surprise at its contents and satisfaction at its cordiality. Lincoln did not often sign himself "Your friend," and his reference to the failure of the Sumter

expedition as nothing worse than an annoyance was
the last thing Fox could have expected. True, he had
never anticipated failure, as the letter indicated; but
as a man of keen perceptions the former navy officer
probably wondered if the President was hinting at
something he did not wish to express in so many words.
Perhaps the exact phrasing of Lincoln's enigmatic
reply to his protest against the short time for fitting
out the expedition came back to him: "You will best
fulfill your duty to your country by making the attempt." The thought that the expedition had never
been intended to succeed may suddenly have occurred
to Fox. If so, it must have come as quite a shock to him.

Fox's 1865 report furnished more interesting information. When the shells had begun falling over the
doomed fort, the captains of the *Pawnee* and *Harriet
Lane* had shown laudable eagerness to defy the shore
batteries and rush to Anderson's assistance, something Fox had not mentioned in his earlier report. He
now admitted that it was he who had restrained them.
"I advised both . . . to go close in to the . . . channel
and anchor. . . ." This dodge, however, only postponed matters, for when morning came Rowan wanted
to "share the fate of his brethren of the Army," and
Fox had to meet the issue squarely. He calmly told
the captain "that the government did not expect such
gallant sacrifice," and then followed it with a remark
which really let the cat out of the bag. The government, he declared, had "settled maturely upon the
policy indicated in the instructions to myself," and he
would take full responsibility for carrying them out.
That Fox had received private instructions—what they

were he did not divulge—was startling news. Both
Cameron and Welles had ordered the use of force if
necessary. A contrary policy, settled maturely or
otherwise, could have been dictated by no one but the
President. This could only mean that Lincoln had
secretly directed Fox to keep the warships from entering the harbor, thereby making the use of force impossible. Fox was quite agreeable, because he had never
intended to use the warships for anything but a base,
leaving to him "as the author of the plan the actual
operations of relief." He had said so plainly in a letter
to Scott as early as February 8.[12] But from there on his
aims and those of Lincoln apparently had tended in
different directions. While Fox did not want to share
the glory with the Navy, he had been eager to supply
Anderson, believing it to be the express purpose of
the expedition. Lincoln, on the other hand, was not
only anxious to keep the ships out of the harbor for
fear that they might start an armed conflict, but was
equally anxious to keep the supplies out of the fort,
because its surrender by April 12 was part of his master
plan. Fox had not been allowed to share this secret, but
his wings had to be clipped by some means or other.
The details the President had left to Seward, who used
the simple expedient of detaching the *Powhatan* with
her indispensable boats, sailors and fighting launches.

The mystery surrounding the inactivity of the fleet
thus was cleared up, but it must be regretted that Fox
did not reveal the gist of the secret orders he had
received. Nevertheless, from what transpired subsequently, some deductions are possible. Aside from
ordering that the warships be kept outside the bar, Lin-

coln had probably tried subtly to forestall Fox's resentment at finding that, in the absence of the *Powhatan,* he could not send provisions to the beleaguered fort. The President may have remarked that small boats were almost certain to be sunk, but that even if so they would serve a worth-while purpose by putting the Confederates in the wrong for shooting at unarmed vessels bound on a mission of mercy.

One more point still remains obscure. How did it happen that Fox, a civilian, had been chosen to carry out a secret policy of the government? On second thought there is nothing strange about it. Instead of being an obstacle to his appointment, his civilian status had worked in his favor. A civilian was not bound by army rules and need not report on confidential missions to anyone but the President.

When Fox received Lincoln's letter of May 1, he had the good sense to see that it was politically explosive. He sent a copy of it to his wife, but admonished her not to make it public. *"Under no circumstances* is any mention of it *whatever* to get into the papers," he wrote. "The whole history of the affair is in able hands and in due time will appear. . . ."[13]

The able hands, it may be assumed, were the President's, and the reason for secrecy was that the letter exposed the spuriousness of the relief expedition. But the "due time" which Fox held out as a lure to future chroniclers never did appear, and the "whole history of the affair" still is nebulous; at any rate, none of the principal participants has seen fit to tell it in its entirety.

The most mysterious part of Lincoln's letter to Fox, aside from his reference to the failure of the Sumter expedition as merely annoying, is his admission that he had anticipated this possibility, yet was satisfied with the result. Why? The whisperers claimed that it strengthened their case: he had tricked the Confederates into firing the first shot. In the South this belief never was abandoned, but in the North it gradually went into semi-oblivion for want of additional fuel. Not until the late eighties was it reawakened, curiously enough, through Lincoln's former secretaries; but their opinion, although bluntly expressed, received scant notice. Some forty years later the whispers received an impetus which created a livelier interest. In 1927 the diary of Senator Browning, one of Lincoln's oldest friends, was bared to the public. Found in it was the record of a remark the President had made to him on July 3, 1861. That evening Browning had called at the White House, and upon his return wrote down what had transpired. The gist of it was that Lincoln had told him:

The plan succeeded. They attacked Sumter—it fell, and thus, did more service than it otherwise could.[14]

These words were widely accepted as definite proof of Lincoln's duplicity,[15] yet it is hard to say why they stirred up any excitement, for there was nothing in them that had not been known before. They did not differ materially from those in the account of his former secretaries, nor from what the President had written to Fox—that, despite its failure, the expedition had

"advanced the cause of the country," which was only
another way of saying that the fall of Fort Sumter "did
. . . service." To Fox he intimated that the outcome
of the relief attempt would have been satisfactory
whether successful or not, and to Browning he declared that it had succeeded and thereby had served
its purpose. Again there is no important variance between the two versions.

Several years previously another allusion to Lincoln's attitude regarding Sumter had appeared in
print, but had fallen flat. In 1918 the Naval History
Society published the *Confidential Correspondence of
Gustavus Vasa Fox.* In a letter to Blair, dated April 17,
1861, Fox had made an odd statement while relating a
talk he had had with Anderson after the surrender. It
seems that during this conversation Lincoln's words
evidently had become plain to him. "I also explained
the reasons for holding the fort," he wrote.[16] ". . . I told
the Major how anxious the Prest was that they (S.C.)
should stand before the civilized world as having fired
upon bread. . . ."[17]

Lincoln's remarks to Fox and Browning, taken in
conjunction with his May 1 letter and the accounts of
Nicolay and Hay, show that he was not disappointed
about the termination of the Sumter venture, that in
fact he was pleased with it. Even so, this does not
prove that he deliberately jockeyed the Confederates
into a cul-de-sac from which they had to shoot their
way out; nor does it disprove it. What it does prove
is that he had been fully prepared to deal with the
only alternative he could see, should his Sumter peace
plan miscarry. This alternative was war. He may

even have wished the plan to fail, as he never had been completely convinced that Seward's policy was sound. If so, more honor is due him for trying it out, and for exploring what he considered a forlorn hope to avert war.

Out of this hodgepodge of facts and conjectures a few justifiable conclusions emerge.

Fox's so-called relief expedition was a make-believe affair and had been destined to fail.

Lincoln had honestly tried to bring about Anderson's peaceful surrender.

He had not willfully entrapped the Confederates into firing on Fort Sumter, but was pleased with the action.

While war was not an unavoidable consequence of the bombardment, Lincoln accepted it in preference to a continuance of uncertainty. He simply reverted to the view he had expressed to Browning in February, that a short war, fought quickly, would prevent a long war later on. He had staked everything on his belief that victory would be won in a matter of months, and so far there was nothing in the picture to disturb this illusion. The North was girding its loins, and he expected that before long the conflict would be decided in its favor.

6

Lincoln Turns Autocrat

THE PRESIDENTIAL PROCLAMATION of April 15 was accepted by both sides as a declaration of war, and has been so construed ever since. However, this may not have been its intent, for Lincoln had left two tiny cracks open for a peaceable settlement: he gave the "combinations opposing the laws" twenty days to obey his "command" to disperse, and said that the militia "probably" would first be used to repossess seized Federal properties, which indicated that he had not reached a decision on this vital issue.

The possibility that the proclamation was meant as a genuine peace offer may be ruled out. The harsh tone and definite time limit, both in the conventional style of an ultimatum, virtually assured its rejection; worse than that, it was apt to turn the cotton states into active enemies. Yet Lincoln disclosed to them what he proposed to do, and then mitigated his threat by inserting the word "probably." Why?

A possible explanation for this extraordinary proceeding is that Lincoln, while officially addressing the
Confederates, was in reality aiming his promulgation
at the border states and at his Northern constituents.
So far as the Confederates were concerned, he had
already decided, after the collapse of his peace effort,
that a brief war was the best way to clear the atmosphere. But he may still have hoped to avoid actual
bloodletting, for the threat to repossess and then hold
all the lost Federal property located in the midst of a
hostile population was an obvious absurdity. Blockad-
ing the ports of the seceded states and gathering an
army might be sufficient to bring the Confederates to
terms.

The proclamation, he may have hoped, would solve
two vexatious problems. For one, it would placate
both opposing Northern factions, because the word
"probably" should please the peaceable Northerners
by hinting at an eleventh-hour effort to avert war,
while the conditional threat to use force should appease the war party. Its second and more important
purpose, however, may have been to keep the border
states from joining the Confederacy, for it provided a
twenty-day interim, which would give the Southern
Unionists time to nurse and fan Union sentiment in
their localities. The word "probably" should give them
help and encouragement in their efforts.

If this was the President's plan, it did not work out
at all. In the North only the warmongers were made
happy by the proclamation. The peace party simply
folded up, its counsel for patience and reflection
drowned in the feverish cry, "On to Richmond!" Nor

did the border states react in the way Lincoln had
hoped. The Unionists, so far as they did not switch
over to the Secessionists, lost their influence overnight.
No one was impressed by Lincoln's endeavor to soften
the ultimatum by his qualifying adverb; in fact,
there is no record that anyone, then or at any time
afterward, paid the slightest attention to it, although
as an experienced lawyer Lincoln never would have
inserted the word without a definite purpose. To the
masses a call to arms spelled war, and never mind the
ifs, buts and probablies. Nothing could have satisfied
the border states but a clean-cut declaration that the
troops would be used exclusively for defensive purposes; but repossessing Federal property within the
Confederacy certainly was anything but that. Repossession and invasion were plainly inseparable, and
both were fighting words. With a unanimity born of
resentment and wounded pride, the majority of the
border states closed ranks with the Deep South and
accepted the challenge to redeem their solemn pledge
of meeting coercion with armed resistance. In the
excitement of the moment the infeasibility of repossessing Federal property in their midst was completely lost
sight of.

Lincoln was never at his best when he had to act
hurriedly, and in drafting the proclamation he not only
had acted in extreme haste, but had spurned the opinion of his official advisers, some of whom might have
foreseen its fatal consequences. His action accomplished in a few hours something the Confederates
themselves had not been able to accomplish in two
months: it solidified most of the South into one great

brotherhood, and led to a more widespread disintegration of the Union than had seemed possible a few
days before. But the most serious of Lincoln's mis-
calculations was his assumption that all the Southern
leaders would abide by their stipulation to submit
secession to a popular vote. It must have come as a
terrible shock to him when the Virginia Convention,
without waiting for the referendum which it had itself
set for May 23, passed an ordinance of secession on
April 17, only two days after the issuance of the proclamation. Baldwin had been right: Virginia, the key
border state, had gone out with the first gunshot. It
was the last thing Lincoln had expected or desired.
Too late it was brought home to him that the proclamation had been a fateful and irretrievable error. In
place of a short conflict, which could have been largely
waged with words and saber-rattling against a government whose main territory was out of reach, he suddenly found himself confronted with the likelihood of
a full-fledged war, in which a populous state whose
boundary lay within view of the White House was
bound to play an important role.

Nevertheless, the situation was not altogether hope-
less. So far the other border states had stood by their
resolve to submit secession to popular vote, and might
yet be held in line. The President saw an opportunity
to isolate Virginia from the rest of the South, and attempted to achieve this without delay. His most pressing problem, however, was to hold on to Maryland,
whose loyalty was essential for the safety of the capital. In full appreciation of this danger, he set out to
do what he now saw he should have done in the first

place: explain that his call for troops was a purely precautionary measure. Direct appeals to the remaining border states must wait. In the meantime they would understand, he hoped, that what he was about to tell the Marylanders applied to them as well.

The President let only three days pass before he addressed a delegation from Baltimore, headed by Mayor George W. Brown, who quoted the President as having said that *"the protection of Washington . . . was the sole object of concentrating troops there; . . . that none . . . were intended for any purpose . . . aggressive as against the Southern states."*[1] Another committee from Baltimore was similarly assured: "I have no desire to invade the South; but I must have troops to defend this capital."[2] And on April 24 he wrote a confidential letter to the noted Maryland lawyer Reverdy Johnson: "I do say the sole purpose of bringing troops here is to defend this Capital. I do say I have no purpose to invade Virginia with them or any other troops, as I understand the word invasion. But suppose Virginia . . . strikes us, are we not to strike back . . . ?"[3]

These assurances, if embodied originally in his proclamation and not added as a transparent afterthought, might have kept the entire uncommitted South in the Union. But their omission, combined with the brusque phrasing of the proclamation, more than offset Lincoln's belated mollifying words. How could repossession be brought about without invasion, no matter how the President understood the word? The border states answered this question promptly and unequivocally.

Arkansas and Tennessee seceded in the first days of May, and North Carolina followed on the twenty-third, bringing the total number of Confederate states to eleven. The defection of four additional states changed the situation, calamitously. War with the cotton states alone might have ended swiftly, perhaps need not have been fought at all because, aside from their geographical position and the growing dissensions between themselves, their economic structure was too weak to sustain them as a political unit. Moreover, the border states, caught in an uncomfortable position, would have exerted a pacifying influence. These favorable factors now had been eliminated, and with them perished the expectation of ending the war with an army of 75,000 men.

Neither Lincoln himself nor anyone since ever explained the "probably" in the proclamation; but Lincoln did furnish an explanation of what invasion meant to him, and it was not conducive to peace. On May 24, only a few hours after the last of the seceding states had broken its tie with the Union, he ordered the occupation of Arlington and of Alexandria. A short time later he directed McDowell's army to advance on Manassas. After this the fiction that an invasion was not an invasion could no longer be maintained. Lincoln could not claim to be striking back at Virginia, because Virginia had not struck at anyone, nor had she threatened Washington. The only possible conclusion is that after his promises to the people of Baltimore had failed of their purpose, Lincoln considered them void and felt free to wage aggressive war. He never again referred to his promise or showed the slightest hesitancy in invading Southern territory.

The entire picture had changed. Lincoln's army of 75,000 men suddenly looked puny. He wished he had followed Douglas' advice to raise an initial army of 200,000, and his uneasiness was augmented by Scott's warnings against sending insufficiently trained men into combat. His call to arms now emerged as what it was: a half-measure which, instead of serving its end, would prove a costly and irretrievable blunder.

The outlook was discouraging, but Lincoln was not a man to give way to panic. He would meet the changed situation as best he could. The short term of the volunteers was particularly impeding, but he would try, despite Scott's objection, to gain a decisive victory before the enlistments expired. In the meantime he would build up a bigger fighting force of a more permanent character. In carrying out his program, however, he ran into grave constitutional obstacles. He found, as others had found before him, that wars cannot be waged under the laws and moral standards of peace. His right to call out the militia for the purpose assigned to it already had been questioned. Douglas had argued against it on the floor of the Senate, and Congress had supported his contention. Under Buchanan's administration a bill empowering the President to use the militia for retaking the lost Federal forts had been recommended to the House of Representatives by the Military Committee, but it was shelved.[4] Subsequently another bill was introduced to give the President the right of employing the militia to suppress insurrections. It too was killed, probably with Lincoln's approval.[5] But whatever the legal status of his call for troops, there was no doubt whether he had the right to increase the armed forces beyond the numbers fixed by statute; this was the exclusive privilege of Congress. Nevertheless, the President infringed it by asking for 42,000 three-year volunteers, while simultaneously increasing the regular Army by 22,000 and the Navy by 18,000 recruits. In issuing these orders he openly and knowingly violated the Constitution, yet the addition of four states to the Confederacy gave him little choice. Though Congress was not in session, he felt certain that when it met it would sanction his measure in view of the existing emergency. No one denied that an emergency existed, but his critics pointed out that it was his own proclamation which had created it and that he was deliberately prolonging it by his delay in convening Congress.

The strengthening of the armed forces was Lincoln's first undisputed violation of the Constitution. It was not his last, for it is the inexorable rule of lawlessness that each transgression leads to another, until the transgressor is caught in a morass of illegality from which there is no escape.

The next infraction was not slow in forthcoming. Because eastern Maryland was honeycombed with Southern sympathizers, and the seat of the government was still insecure, the President ordered a suspension of the writ of habeas corpus in the affected area. Chief Justice Taney of the United States Supreme Court condemned this action as unlawful, clothing his censure in scathing words. If the suspension were allowed to stand, he said, the United States no longer had a government by law; the life, liberty and property of every citizen were at the mercy of army officers.[6] When Lincoln sought the advice of his Attorney General he received a reply which could not have been worded more ambiguously by the Delphian oracle. The President, Bates said, being commander-in-chief, rules in peace and commands in war within the limits of the Constitution.[7] But there was nothing ambiguous in his prediction that the suspension, if brought before the courts, would be held unconstitutional. Lincoln disregarded the warning of the two legal luminaries. The law of self-preservation outweighed man-made statutes, and the unlawful edict was allowed to stand.

The President next usurped the rights of the legislative branch by disbursing monies without Congressional appropriations. Subsequently he admitted he had acted illegally, but he offered the lame excuse that "not a dollar of the public funds . . . was either lost or wasted."[8] Would the lawyer Lincoln, pleading for a client who had dipped into someone else's cashbox, have argued that the theft had been no crime because the money had been used economically and for a worthy purpose?

One of Lincoln's dictatorial acts must have haunted his sleep. On April 19 he proclaimed a blockade of all Southern ports in the seceded states. Blockades are on the list of legitimate war measures, but three out of seven Justices of the Supreme Court decided that the power to declare war was invested solely in Congress. By a single vote Lincoln escaped the humiliation of having all his war orders antedating the approval of Congress invalidated.[9] The narrowness of the decision came close to being a judicial spanking.

The current which was swirling Lincoln along the path of autocracy rushed on relentlessly. Suspension of the writ brought in its wake the arbitrary arrests of private citizens. Often these arrests were made only on mere suspicion or because of denunciation by spiteful neighbors. Homes were entered at night and their owners spirited away to military prisons. Members of the Maryland legislature, which was about to meet, were thrown into jail. The files of telegraph offices were ransacked for messages expressed in privacy during the past year, allegedly to be scrutinized to detect subversive activities, but more likely to earmark people antagonistic to the administration.[10] The execution of these decrees was delegated to underlings who, under the direction of the erstwhile conciliatory Seward, went berserk in their newly acquired despotic power.[11]

The correspondent of the London *Times*, William H. Russell, was appalled by the submissiveness with which the people accepted this throwback to a worse imperialism than the one against which their forefathers had rebelled. After the arrest of the Maryland legislators he told his paper that "the news . . . has not produced the smallest effect here: so easily do men . . . bend to arbitrary power, and so rapidly do all guarantees disappear in a revolution."[12] He might have added that if there was a revolution it was an unusual one— it had been fomented not by the people, but by their rulers. Russell also overlooked the fact that the people were in a condition of shock. They could not believe that such infractions of the Bill of Rights could be perpetrated by their President, who had constantly stressed his reverence for the Constitution; nor could they believe that this could happen in an allegedly free country, and in an age which liked to call itself the Enlightened Nineteenth Century. A joke was warmed up which had been making the rounds in Buchanan's time. The President, it ran, was willing to "give up a part, and, if necessary, *the whole* of the Constitution, *to preserve the remainder!*"[13]

Horace Greeley stabbed with a sharp pen at what he considered ill-disguised dictatorship. He wrote to the President:

I never doubted . . . that you desire . . . to re-establish the . . . authority . . . of the Republic. I intended only to raise this question—Do you propose to do this by recognizing, obeying and enforcing the laws, or by ignoring, disregarding, and in effect defying them?[14]

Since Greeley was a power to be reckoned with, no action was taken against him for his frank and courageous protest.

Lincoln's minister to Spain, Carl Schurz, who had left Germany in order to escape tyranny, conveyed his troubled feelings to Seward, but as a diplomat he had to use guarded language:

It is exceedingly difficult to make Europeans understand . . . that the same means of repression which are of so baneful a memory to most European nations

. . . are found necessary to prop the Federal Government; and that the latter . . . is with rapid strides approaching the line which separates democratic government from . . . arbitrary despotism.[15]

The *London Saturday Review* was incensed about "the arrest of the newly elected members of the [Maryland] legislative assembly before they had had any time to meet . . . because President Lincoln conceived that they might . . . do acts at variance with his interpretation of the American Constitution. . . ." The editor then sneered at "the land of the free, . . . in which electors may not vote for fear of arrest, . . . judges may not execute the law for fear of dismissal—in which . . . advocates are threatened with imprisonment and hostile newspapers are suppressed."[16]

Perhaps the most cogent condemnation of these illegal measures came from two of the principal culprits themselves. Three years later, in rare self-denunciation, Seward confided to the artist Carpenter that the Cabinet had been guilty of political crimes which might have brought all of its members to the scaffold.[17] This was trenchant criticism, but Secretary of War Stanton, who had succeeded Seward as head of the Secret Service, was not less outspoken. His arbitrary arrests, he remarked cynically, if successfully prosecuted, would have kept him in prison for a thousand years.[18]

In justice to Lincoln it should be noted that his illegal steps were a logical part of his endeavor to shorten the conflict. The unfettered actions of a fifth column would lengthen it, hence had to be held in

check at any cost; and since the Constitution offered
no remedy for a situation which its signers had not
foreseen, it had to be ignored for the time being. A
frank admission to this effect, however, and an early
convening of Congress, would have gone a long way
toward silencing the strictures which were heaped on
the administration. Lincoln never gave a reason for his
dilatoriness in calling the legislators into session, and
even at this late day no explanation for it has been
offered by his apologists.

As the conflict progressed far beyond the anticipated
three months, and the temporary suspension of the
Constitution assumed a semipermanent status, the
President found it increasingly difficult to defend his
arbitrary acts. The question whether the exigencies
of war gave the government the right to transcend the
law became the subject of heated debates. For a time
Lincoln took no part in them, but the pressure of
public opinion finally made him break his silence. He
contended that the Constitution invested him with
"the law of war in time of war," a dogma which Thad-
deus Stevens previously had thus announced in Congress: "I thought the time had come, when the
laws of war were to govern . . . when constitutions,
if they stood in the way, . . . had no right to inter-
vene."[19] The erudite Senator Sumner presented the
same idea in more stilted form:

In seeking to fasten upon [war] the restraints of the
Constitution, you repeat the ancient tyranny which
compelled its victims to fight in chains. Glorious as it

is that the citizen is surrounded by the safeguards of
the Constitution, yet this rule is superseded by war
which brings into being other rights which know no
master.[20]

Attorney General Bates disagreed wholeheartedly
with this view. He looked with disdain at those who
arrogated to themselves unwarranted authority.
"When the constitution fails them," he scoffed in his
diary, "they have only to say 'this is a time of war—
and war gives all needed powers.' "[21]

Dissenting voices rose on the floor of Congress too,
and they were not confined to the opposition party.
Said Republican Senator Trumbull of Illinois: "Necessity is the plea of tyrants; and if our Constitution
ceases to operate the moment a person charged with
its observance thinks there is a necessity to violate it,
it is of little value."[22] As Trumbull was chairman of
the Senate Judiciary Committee, his words carried
weight. The ultra-anti-administration Congressman
Vallandigham, waxing impatient at mere legalistic discussions, denounced further oratory as a waste of time.
In January 1862 he introduced a resolution which
went to the heart of the controversy:

Resolved, That whoever shall affirm that it is compe-
tent for this House, or any other authority, *to establish
a Dictatorship in the United States* . . . will be guilty
of *a high crime against the constitution and the
Union.* . . .[23]

The resolution was defeated, but the attacks on Lin-

coln became so vehement that he thought it advisable
to define his standpoint. In time of war, he insisted,
the Constitution was different from the Constitution in
time of peace, and endowed him with extralegal powers of which he alone was the judge. This interpretation met with derision, providing the occasion for a
free exchange of verbal blows. In May 1863 General
Burnside had arrested Vallandigham for an allegedly
insurrectory speech, and a Democratic convention in
Albany challenged the President in stinging terms:

This assumption of power . . . not only abrogates the
right of people to assemble, . . . the liberty of speech
and of the press, the right of trial by jury, . . . and the
privilege of *habeas corpus,* but it strikes . . . at the
supremacy of law. . . . These safeguards . . . have
stood the test for seventy-six years . . . and [we] bid
defiance to any arm that would move us. . . .[24]

Lincoln's reply was calm, but determined:

. . . The resolutions . . . assert . . . that certain military
arrests and proceedings following them . . . are unconstitutional. I think they are not. . . . Thoroughly im-
bued with a reverence for the guaranteed rights of
individuals, I was slow to adopt the strong measures,
which by degrees I have been forced to regard as being within the exceptions of the Constitution. . . .[25]

Lincoln was wrong in two of his allegations. First,
he had not been slow to adopt strong measures, but
had put them into effect immediately after his proc-

lamation. Furthermore, he had promised that he
would recognize no exception to the Constitution but
would obey it as it was, not as he wished it to be.
Perhaps he sensed the inconsistency of his position,
for he swerved from the legal aspect of the debate to
common-sense arguments as to the ability of civil
courts to function in time of war. "A jury," he said,
"too frequently has at least one member, more ready
to hang the panel than to hang the traitor."[26] A former
trial lawyer was winking at other lawyers who had
gone through similar experiences, and expected them
to understand him.

Lincoln then propounded an amazing new principle:

Habeas corpus does not discharge men . . . and its suspension is allowed by the Constitution on purpose that
men may be arrested . . . *who can not be proved to be
guilty of defined crime*, "when . . . the public Safety
may require it" . . . arrests are made, not so much for
what has been done, *as for what probably would be
done.*[27]

A Wisconsin editor reading this startling theory ut-
tered a cry of anguish. "Oh, Moses," he exclaimed,
"what a rule!"[28]

The members of the committee which had drafted
the resolution were not swayed by Lincoln's rejoinder.
They took particular exception to the reasoning that
men could be imprisoned for a crime which they had
not committed but might commit in the future. Ac-

cording to the President, so the committee protested
angrily, a man could be lawfully imprisoned " for the
crime of silence, of speech and opinion."[29]

Illustrating his novel doctrine, Lincoln pointed out
that if Lee, Johnston and other men holding high posi-
tions in the Confederacy had been seized at the out-
set, "the insurgent cause would be much weaker."[30]
Nevertheless, the President evidently had little faith
in his case, for he tried to strengthen it by one of the
homely similes in which he excelled, and which were
among his most potent dialectic weapons. "I can no
more be persuaded," he wrote, "that the government
can . . . take no strong measure in time of rebellion . . .
than I can be . . . that a particular drug is not good
medicine for a sick man, because it . . . [is] not good
food for a well one."[31] With equal adroitness he tried to
allay apprehension that the people might permanently
lose their peaceful rights. He did not believe that a
man "could contract so strong an appetite for emetics
during temporary illness, as to persist in feeding upon
them through the remainder of his healthful life."[32]

On June 29, 1863, Lincoln, as if tired of juristical
subtleties, finally stated his position without mincing
his words:

You ask . . . whether I really claim that I may override
all the guaranteed rights of individuals . . . when I may
choose to say the public safety requires it. . . . The
Constitution contemplates the question as likely to
occur . . . but it does not . . . declare who is to decide
it. . . . I think the man whom . . . the people have . . .

made the commander-in-chief . . . is the man who holds the power. . . .[33]

This was straight hitting, and left no room for doubt. Lincoln held the power, and intended to use it.

In time the Supreme Court decided the right and wrong of this controversy. In the famous Milligan case the majority of the court gave Lincoln's interpretation a merciless tongue-lashing. What made its decision especially noteworthy was that it was read by Lincoln's friend and former campaign manager, David Davis, a man Lincoln himself had appointed to the Supreme Court bench. The Court declared:

The Constitution of the United States is a law for rulers and people, equally in war and peace. . . . No doctrine involving more pernicious consequences was ever invented . . . than that any of its provisions can be suspended during any of the great exigencies. . . . Such a doctrine leads directly to anarchy or despotism. . . .[34]

By then, however, the war was over, and Lincoln was in his grave.

Looking back on these troublesome days, it is clear that Lincoln was facing problems which had no easy solution. On December 13, 1860, he had declared that "It is the duty of the President to . . . maintain the existing Government. He cannot entertain any proposition for dissolution or dismemberment. He was not elected for any such purpose."[35] He had publicly and privately reiterated that he would preserve the Union and, if necessary, hold the two sections together by force. He had also promised that he would abide by the Constitution. Unfortunately, these two promises were not compatible in the circumstances; he had to break one or the other, and he chose to give up the Constitution. The inevitable consequence was dictatorship.

There may have been a kernel of truth in Jefferson Davis' remark that Lincoln was a maniac on the subject of an undivided Union; but the Confederate Vice President perhaps showed a better understanding when he said that with Lincoln the Union rose to the sublimity of religious mysticism.[36]

Religious mysticism knows no compromise. What Lincoln stipulated was equal to unconditional surrender, and it helped to prolong the war, the more so because Jefferson Davis, equally determined, would accept nothing short of complete independence for the Southern states. So long as the two rival leaders persisted in their uncompromising, not to say uncompromisable demands—and both did persist in them to the last—a negotiated peace was impossible, much as the people on both sides may have prayed for it. But the people had long since found out that, the outward trimmings of democratic governments notwithstanding, the war had turned both sections into autocracies where *vox populi* had been stilled, and the word of their rulers had become the law of the land.

7

Congress Meets

THE COUNTRY WONDERED what action Congress would take when at last it met on July 4. Would the people's representatives rise in wrath? Lincoln did not think so, and looked forward to the session without qualms. The Republicans controlled both Houses, and he knew well that since the fighting was getting into full swing, Congress could do nothing but sustain him. As a Congressman he himself had pronounced the Mexican War unjust, yet had consistently voted in support of it. Few had dared to do otherwise; few would dare do otherwise now.

The President's message turned out to be one of the poorest he ever delivered. He began by stating truthfully that he had exhausted all peaceful steps before using force, and that he had sought only to hold those public places which had not already been wrested from the government. As to the adjustment of other issues, he would have relied on time, discussions and the ballot box. This statement must have set the lawmakers to thinking. If Lincoln had regarded neither secession itself nor the previous loss of a great many public places as a *casus belli*, why then had the addition of a single fort to the list precluded the same peaceable adjustment, especially as the other of the two places not already wrested from the government had remained in its possession?

The President tried to dispel these misgivings so as "to keep the case . . . free from the power of ingenious sophistry." He explained that "then and there the assailants of the government began the conflict of arms, without a gun in sight or in expectancy to return their fire, save only the few in the fort. . . ." Had he forgotten the guns of the warships which indisputably had been in sight as well as in expectancy? Or did he believe that his listeners had forgotten them?

Lincoln was playing with words when he declared that Fort Sumter had been bombarded "without even awaiting the arrival of the provisioning expedition." True, the fleet had not yet arrived, but it obviously was assembling, and its approach had been reported by Confederate scout boats. In stating that the garrison of the fort "could by no possibility have committed aggression," he ignored Anderson's threat, made earlier in the year, that by turning his guns on the harbor he could close it to all shipping.[1] Charleston itself lay beyond the range of his batteries, but obstruction of the city's maritime commerce would have been almost as ruinous to it as a bombardment.

Lincoln handled himself well, however, when he discussed whether a democracy could uphold its territorial integrity against domestic foes; whether discontented individuals could break up their government instead of relying for redress on means provided by the Constitution. This question, in his opinion, embraced more than the fate of the American nation; it concerned "the whole family of man." It was the keystone of Lincoln's political philosophy, and he presented it with the eloquence characteristic of him whenever he spoke from deep conviction.

"So viewing the issue," Lincoln continued, "no choice was left but to call out the war power of the government. . . ." Was there really no choice left? Why had he not held to his intention of relying on time, discussions and the ballot box, when the country stood most in need of them?

The President also mentioned his abortive plan to evacuate Fort Sumter but hold Fort Pickens. He referred to the *quasi armistice* at Pensacola of which, he said, he had heard "only too vague and uncertain rumors to fix attention." He neglected to say why he had not investigated rumors of such import, although well-informed officials of the preceding administration had been at his beck and call. It would have been more forthright to state frankly that he had been aware of the truce, but had broken it because he needed a strong position at the Gulf before yielding the Charleston fort. His honest effort to maintain peace did not need a farfetched justification.

The President next ventured into dangerous ground. His call for the militia and his proclamation of the blockade, he averred, were "believed to be strictly legal." He hoped Congress would ratify his call for volunteers and the large addition to the regular armed forces, "whether strictly legal or not." He admitted that the legality and propriety of these measures were being denied, but he answered this accusation by asserting that if he had violated the Constitution he had done so under what appeared to be a popular demand and public necessity. The public necessity was questionable, but there certainly had been no popular demand for war, and still less one for arbitrary arrests or the suspension of the writ.

On the other hand, one must admire Lincoln's integrity in calling attention to the obvious incongruity that an official sworn to "take care that the laws be faithfully executed" should be the one to have violated them. But, Lincoln asked, since *all* the laws were being resisted by a third of the nation, was it wrong to break *one* if otherwise the government would go to pieces?

To claim that two wrongs make a right was a poor argument. Lincoln realized it, for it was the only part of his address in which he used involved language, an infallible sign that he was conscious of trying to defend an indefensible issue. He asked clumsily:

Must they [the laws] be allowed to finally fail of execution, even had it been perfectly clear that by the use of the means necessary to their execution, some single law, made in such extreme tenderness to the citizen's liberty that, practically, it relieves more of the guilty than of the innocent, should to a limited extent be violated?

Such muddled verbosity was quite unlike Lincoln's usual clear and beautiful style, but it served well to hide the inherent weakness of his logic. How, for instance, could a law be violated "to a very limited extent?" The President was too good a lawyer not to have inwardly revolted at his own words. In contrast to this prolixity, he was concise in his plea to make the contest "short and decisive." This was the aim and hope of his war policy, and in stressing it he was in desperate earnest. A favorable result at an early stage, he reasoned sensibly, would be worth ten times what it would cost later.

At the very end of his message the President made a strange admission. "The executive . . . sincerely hopes," he said, "that your views and action may so accord with his as to assure all faithful citizens who have been disturbed in their rights, of a certain and speedy restoration to them, under the Constitution and the laws."

After Lincoln's repeated pleas that his actions had not been unconstitutional, this climactic confession came as a surprise. His pledge that the invaded rights of the people would speedily be restored to them rested, of course, on the premise that the war would not last long. This supposition was the very core of his policy, and it would have been well had he made it the main thesis of his address rather than let it dangle at the tail end of it. Here was his great opportunity to lay before the people the foundation of his autocratic conduct since the fall of Fort Sumter. The three months which he had set as the time limit for the war were not yet over; an army was being assembled, enthusiasm was still running high. If even at this late hour he had invited the people, as represented by Congress, to share with him the guilt of defying the

Constitution and adopting the harsh, illegal measures
for the sake of internal security and a quick victory, he
would have saved himself much justified criticism and
future embarrassment.

As it was, Congress did not take kindly to his speech.
His secretaries conceded that the only clause which
was greeted with hearty applause was the proposal
to make the war short and decisive.[2] Though a joint
resolution was introduced to legalize Lincoln's "extraordinary" acts, it did not pass, probably because Congress resented being coerced into voting approval of
things already done without its consent. The word
"usurpation" often crept into the debates. Many members, suspecting that Lincoln had deliberately delayed
the session so as to be free from possible opposition,
agreed with the *London Spectator,* that the "President . . . thinks like a European sovereign."[3] Congress
showed its anger by postponing ratification of Lincoln's war edicts to the end of the session. Finally,
however, it bowed to the inevitable, as Lincoln had
known all along it could not help doing.

The time for speeches was over, the time for action
had arrived. While Congress was in session the Battle
of Bull Run was being fought, the battle on which
Lincoln had staked his hope for the end of the war.
Its outcome was a fearful blow to him, as it was to the
entire North. Henry R. Raymond, editor of the *New
York Times,* echoing the President's thought, was dis-
consolate. "The most sanguine expectations of a
prompt and decisive victory had been universally entertained," he wailed; "and the actual issue first

revealed to the people the prospect of a long and bloody war."[4] Overnight Lincoln's calculation had been smashed into bits. He blamed himself for the debacle, for it was he who had prompted Scott to strike before the Army was ready.[5] The general had protested against haste, but his hand had been forced by Lincoln, who still thought of the days when wars were often ended by a single victory. Bull Run, though, opened his eyes, for he perceived clearly that it was more than a lost battle. It foreshadowed the outline of future events: the war would not be decided by one battle, probably not by two or three. Moreover, victory was by no means so certain as it had appeared a few weeks before. He, the Blairs and his other advisers had misjudged the prospects, had misjudged them disastrously. The Northern press also had been dead wrong. Nevertheless, he was ready to take the blame, for it was not his habit to unload blame on other shoulders. Taking immediate steps to remedy the situation was imperative, however. Perhaps a change in army leadership would bring with it a change in fortune. Scott went out, McClellan took his place, and new hopes arose that peace would come before the year was over. But disappointment followed disappointment. Week after week saw Lincoln's vision of a short war whittled away by cold actualities. The ninety-day men left, voluntary enlistment lagged. In the first flush of excitement large masses could have been enrolled for the duration, but the opportunity had not been seized and it never reappeared. Conscription with all its attending evils was looming on the horizon. Lincoln had tried to achieve a speedy victory by dictatorial severity at home and a military coup in the field. Neither had been successful. He would have to devise other means to gain his end. It was his war; he had started it, it was up to him to end it. But how?

8

Lincoln Evolves a
New Peace Plan

LINCOLN'S REASONING was at all times clear, exhaustive and self-critical. He realized that, since there was no promise of attaining an early peace by fighting, a different approach was in order. With this conclusion firmly in mind he abandoned his hope to re-establish the Union by one crushing victory, and for the third time since his inauguration put his brain to work on the solution of the problem. His first plan, to evacuate Fort Sumter, had failed; his second, based on the Army, had fared no better. He now proposed to end the war by removing its cause, slavery. In his inaugural address he had deplored war, because when the shooting was over the underlying causes would still be the same. But they would not be the same if slavery were abolished. His new plan, conceived in the agony of lonely meditation, was far sounder than the preceding ones, for it went to the root of the sectional enmity. In short, he would have the government buy up all slaves, set them free and colonize them. The proposal was simple, fair and, with the exception of the colonization feature, feasible. Selling this idea to the country was Lincoln's next task, and he threw himself into it with zest and vigor. In December 1861 he proceeded to outline the plan in his annual message to Congress, and in doing so moved cautiously toward his goal. He referred to a law enacted four months previously which decreed that "property used for insurrectionary purposes" could be confiscated, and that in such cases the "legal claims of certain persons to the labor and service of certain other persons" became forfeited.[1] This clause made it possible to free slaves in seceded states, so far as the military had brought their territory under Federal control. He now suggested that loyal states might wish to pass similar enactments for their own benefit, in which case all slaves voluntarily released would be accepted in lieu of taxes, or in some other form, and immediately liberated.[2] Since only the border states were affected by this offer, the President addressed himself especially to their representatives. He strengthened his plea by pointing out that "the insurrection and consequent war" had sprung from the controversy over slavery,[3] but weakened it by his simultaneous advocacy of colonization. This was a deplorable error, for it introduced a new complication into a problem already too complex, and made it easy for his opponents to obscure the issue.

Toward the conclusion of his message the President gave expression to his bitterness that the year had been barren of happy results. "The war continues," he said sadly, and then added, "I have been anxious and careful that the . . . conflict . . . shall not degenerate into a violent and remorseless . . . struggle."[4] Fear had begun to arise in his mind that, if not speedily checked, the unleashed passions of war might make reconciliation difficult.

While waiting for Congress to act, Lincoln tried to put a solid foundation under his proposal, choosing Delaware as his testing ground. It seemed particularly well fitted for this purpose. Its representative in Congress, George P. Fisher, was one of his personal friends and a stanch Unionist. The slaves in the state numbered only some 18,000, and could be liberated for comparatively little money.

The President had, in his own hand, written out two carefully considered drafts of the suggested law. According to the first, all Negroes above the age of thirty-five should become free at once. Children born after the statute had been enacted would also be free. All others should be liberated by 1893. The alternate draft, which Lincoln liked better, was substantially identical except that the payments by the Federal government were to be made annually, while the first plan contemplated payment in a lump sum.

Of the two bills only one was introduced, but not in its original form, and the legislators promptly rejected it in vindictive terms. They called it a plot to abolish slavery, claimed that the central government could not legally appropriate funds to buy slaves, said that Delaware knew how to run her own affairs and, as a final stamp of disapproval, scorned the proposal as attempted bribery.[5]

In Washington, Lincoln's program, as outlined in his December 1861 message, encountered a lukewarm reception, but he was not downhearted. With Congress in session, he would have time and opportunity to work on its members.

The border states had valid reasons for their opposition. Confiscation of slaves owned by "insurrectionists" was a tricky affair. Who would decide on a man's loyalty? Furthermore, the execution of the law was to be in the hands of military personnel unacquainted with local conditions. This would not do. The enforcement would have to be left to the state authorities. Aside from these legitimate objections, there was another not openly talked about: the politicians of the affected states were loath to give up any of their privileges.

Lincoln perceived the defects in his plan. On March 6, 1862, he sent a message to Congress, in which he recommended the passing of a joint resolution to the effect that "the government ought to cooperate with any state which adopted gradual abolishment of slavery," by offering the states pecuniary aid. Swerving from the subject for a moment, he let his chagrin come to the fore again. "If . . . resistance continues," he sighed, "the war must also continue."[6] This worrisome thought seemed never to leave him for long.

The March message differed from that of December by omitting the colonization feature and, what was more important, suggested gradual, not sudden, emancipation.[7] The document was businesslike, but it lacked warmth and received scant praise. His broad hints that it was impossible to foresee all the incidents in store for the country, and that "the proposition now made should prove of more value to the states and private persons concerned than all the institutions and [slave] property" did not tend to make his words popular with slaveholders.

To push matters along, Lincoln waited only four days before inviting a group of border-state representatives to the White House for a heart-to-heart talk.[8] He began by pointing out that the war was getting "terrible, wasting and tedious." Then he explained to them his own predicament. Slaves from their districts were constantly drifting into the Union lines, hoping to be protected; but when they were given asylum, the owners complained that their property rights had been invaded. Appealing to the patriotism of the Congressmen, Lincoln explained that if slavery in the border states were abolished, the Confederacy could no longer hope for a change in their allegiance and would stop fighting. He then tried to show his callers that the government had neither the will nor the right to coerce them into accepting his offer, but hoped they would do so voluntarily.

The visitors, however, were not moved. They remained antagonistic. Their arguments were shallow and insincere. A Missouri representative, for example, had read in the *New York Tribune* that slave owners were being forced to choose between voluntary acceptance and compulsion. Anyway, he added foolishly, since slavery was on the road to extinction, why accept compensation? A member from Kentucky doubted the constitutionality of the scheme. It did not occur to him that, once he had received compensation for his slaves, future court decisions could hardly affect him. Someone else from Missouri declared haughtily that the proposal should properly come from the free states, because to ask slaveholders to commit themselves before the offer for buying their slaves had been formally tendered, was putting them into a false position. Others probably felt, although they did not say so, that the way the war was going slaves were apt to prove a better investment in the end than Federal bonds. When the guests left, Lincoln knew that he had wasted his breath. He was still more dismayed when the Radicals of his own party attacked the measure. Thad Stevens called it "the most diluted milk-and-water gruel . . . ever . . . given to the American nation."[9] Nonetheless, the joint resolution passed both Houses by substantial majorities. Only the border states held back.

During one of the following days the President received a party of gentlemen from Massachusetts, who presented him with a whip. He remarked, more in earnest than in jest, that the gift was suggestive, because a great deal of whipping still had to be done. He did not make it clear who had to be whipped, the enemy or the recalcitrant slaveholders or both. Then he again reverted to what had become his theme song. He was looking forward longingly to the days, he said, "when, seated behind a good pair of horses, we can crack our whips and drive through a peaceful, happy and prosperous land."[10]

One of the reasons why the principle of gradual emancipation, despite its attractiveness, met with so little acclaim was that the country had not been prepared for it. Resistance to it was not much different from that with which mediocre men respond to all new ideas, good or bad, because it forces them to shift their thoughts into unaccustomed grooves. Yet the idea was not new with Lincoln. As Congressman he had introduced a bill for limited compensated emancipation. He had suggested it again in 1854 in Peoria,[11] and at Freeport[12] in 1858. He had found then that he was too far ahead of public thinking, and shelved his plan until he embodied it in his March message.

A welcome stimulant was injected into the President's effort by the passage of a law for gradual compensated emancipation of the slaves in the District of Columbia. It went on the books April 16, 1862,[13] but unfortunately the voluntary colonization feature in it pleased the President more than it did the Negroes.

Encouraged by this slight progress, Lincoln made another appeal to the border-state representatives a month later. Using an unauthorized proclamation for emancipation by General Hunter as a steppingstone, he issued a proclamation of his own in which he warned them once more not to remain blind to the signs of the times, to rise above partisan or personal politics by accepting compensated emancipation. In the form in which it had been offered, "the change it contemplates would come gently as the dews of heaven. . . ." Would they not embrace it?[14] But the pathetic appeal evoked no response.

To Mrs. Eliza P. Gurney, a Quaker lady who called

on him, the President poured out his utter discourage-
ment that he was so little understood. "If I had had
my way, . . ." he confided to her, "this war would have
been ended before this; but . . . it still continues."[15]

As the session neared its close and the border states
showed no sign of yielding, Lincoln addressed their
representatives again on July 12, in a final attempt to
change their attitude. He told them they held more
power for good than any other group of its size. He
regretted that they had not voted for his measure in
March because, if they had, "the war now would be
substantially ended." Whether or not this optimism
was justified, no one could deny the cogency of his
argument that "the plan . . . is yet one of the most
potent and swift means of ending" the war. This time
he put the warning about noncompliance into plain
words. Slaves would be liberated anyway by "the
mere incidents of the war," and the owners would have
nothing valuable in their place. Why not sell them,
instead of having the North and South "cut one another's throats"? "You are patriots and statesmen," he
flattered them, "and, . . . I pray you, consider this
proposition. . . . Our . . . country is in great peril, demanding the loftiest views, and boldest action. . . .
To you, more than to any others, the [privilege]
is given, to assure [its happy future] . . . swell that
grandeur, and . . . link your own names therewith
forever."[16] But the representatives of the border states
remained deaf to his plea, and their passive resistance
continued.

Lincoln was driven almost to distraction. In the

privacy of his White House room he began to question both the necessity of the war and his own righteousness. "[God] could have either *saved* or *destroyed* the Union without a human contest," he wrote for his own contemplation. "Yet the contest began. . . . He could give . . . victory to either side any day." Then came the regretful end refrain of all his thinking: "Yet the contest proceeds."[17]

Amid his appeals to reason, to patriotism and to self-interest for the elimination of slavery, Lincoln did not neglect other endeavors to end the war. If a quick peace could not be secured by buying up the slaves, the military efforts would have to be redoubled. But where were the soldiers to come from? Volunteering had ceased, and no lawful means existed to compel enlistments. Lincoln had to fall back on an act of Congress, passed on July 17, 1862, which related to the use of state militia for Federal service. It gave the President no right to force enrollments into the Army; but on August 4, despite the clear language of the law, he issued a draft for 300,000 men, thus putting conscription into effect without Congressional authorization. Even the mild-mannered and strongly pro-Lincoln historian James G. Randall was unusually severe in his condemnation of this dictatorial transgression.[18]

To guard against a public outcry over this unlawful decree, Lincoln issued another equally unlawful proclamation, declaring all persons accused of resisting drafts, of discouraging volunteer enlistments, or of "any disloyal practice" subject to martial law and trial by court-martial or military commissions. At the same time the writ of habeas corpus was suspended over the

entire country.[19] The victims of this new autocratic
act found little consolation in the fact that the Supreme
Court, four years later, declared military commissions
illegal wherever civil courts were functioning without
obstruction.

Faithful Gideon Welles was depressed by Lincoln's
high-handed conduct. The day after this latest decree
was published, he voiced his disapproval. "I question
the wisdom or utility of . . . proclamations striking deep
on great questions," he lamented in his diary.[20] But
he did not oppose the President openly.

The cool reception which the border states had ac-
corded Lincoln's appeals convinced him that further
attempts at persuasion would be useless. Stronger
pressure was necessary to get action. On July 13, the
day following his last plea, he unburdened himself to
two members of his official family. The President,
Welles wrote, had about come to the conclusion that
it was a military necessity to free the slaves.[21] The
germ of forced emancipation, which had lain dormant
in him for some time, was about to break to the sur-
face. On September 22, 1862, he issued his prelim-
inary Emancipation Proclamation. It was to go into
effect on the first of the coming year.

The announcement was greeted with a mixed chorus
of cheers and jeers. Lincoln himself admitted that it
was unconstitutional;[22] he also knew that it would not
free more than a handful of slaves, because it applied
almost exclusively to territory over which he had no
control. Welles characterized it quaintly as "an arbitrary and despotic measure in the cause of free-

dom."[23] Like most others, even he did not seem to perceive that immediate liberation of slaves was not the purpose of the proclamation, but that it would be a powerful instrument in other directions. It would influence public opinion in England, and it would appease the Radicals, both important points in the political set-up. Equally important, if not more so, it should convince the border states that "the incidents of war" were closing in on them. Few people seemed to understand that what Lincoln cared about was not emancipation as such, but its use as a means to end the war. He had explained this with perfect frankness in his famous letter to Horace Greeley. "My paramount object in this struggle," he had asserted, "*is* to save the Union. . . . If I could save the Union without freeing *any* slave I would do it. . . ."[24] Could language have been clearer?

Congress was to meet in December, a month before emancipation became effective, and under the prodding of the proclamation the border-state representatives might now co-operate. Analyzing the situation without prejudice, Lincoln concluded that he had erred in submitting the proposal before he had worked out all its details and could meet every possible objection. He realized that he had put too much stress on his own embarrassing position, in which the border-state politicians were not interested, and that his appeal to their patriotism had been misdirected. He had come to recognize that the real reason for their opposition was fear of interference with their local affairs. This flaw had to be remedied. The financial arrangements too had to be put on a more rational basis, so as to ease the increased tax burden, a burden which had made even his partisans wary, because it was to be borne by all the states, including those which had no slaves to sell.

By December 1862 Lincoln thought he was ready. In his annual message to Congress he crowded his persuasive powers into one heroic effort to have his re-revised plan adopted. Emancipation, he asserted, must be accomplished by compromise, but it should be a compromise between friends of the Union. To cushion the shock of the transition, the liberation of the slaves should be accomplished gradually during the next thirty-seven years. The necessary funds would be raised through bonds, due at the turn of the century. This was the outside limit, however; each state was to have the right of choosing its own date for their redemption. Emancipation, he pointed out, meant confiscation of property, and therefore the North should contribute its part for adequate compensation. Having shared the fruits of slavery, such as sugar and cotton, the North should also share the financial obligations which were to accrue. Moreover, the burden should fall largely on the coming generation, because it would profit equally by the freedom of the Negro race.[25]

In this polished form Lincoln's proposal was eminently equitable, and it could stand up against all reasonable criticism. Spreading the payments over almost forty years would make its acceptance more palatable to the contemporary taxpayers; spreading them over the entire country should pacify the South; and the right of the states to manage all arrangements within their own domains should please the politicians. The privilege of adopting the plan was open to all states, including those which had seceded. If carried out, it would eradicate the cause of the war and bring it rapidly to a close.

While elucidating his ideas in a message to Congress, the President began changing his role from that of the Chief Executive to that of an inspired prophet. He asked:

If . . . with less money . . . we can preserve . . . the Union . . . than we can by the war alone, is it not economical to do it? The aggregate sum necessary for compensated emancipation would be larger. But it would require no ready cash. . . .

He continued:

It is dreaded that the free people will swarm forth and cover the whole land. Are they not already in the land? Will liberation make them any more numerous?

Lincoln now came to the heart of his object—that compensated emancipation would uproot the cause of the war and thereby end it:

The plan would, I am confident, secure peace more speedily and maintain it more permanently than can be done by force alone, while all it would cost . . . would be easier paid than will be the additional cost of the war if we rely solely upon force, [and] it would cost no blood at all.

The plan is proposed as permanent constitutional law. . . . The requisite three fourths of the States will necessarily include seven of the slave States. Their concurrence . . . would end the struggle now and save the Union forever. . . .

Then he spoke over the heads of Congress to the whole nation:

Will not the good people respond to a united and earnest appeal from us? Can we, can they, by any other means so certainly or so speedily assure these vital objects?

At the close of his message Lincoln rose to great oratorical heights.

Fellow-citizens, *we* cannot escape history. We . . . will be remembered in spite of ourselves. . . . We know how to save the Union. . . . Other means may succeed; this could not fail. The way is plain . . . if followed the world will forever applaud and God must forever bless.

Even the hypercritical Sumner wrote that he remembered nothing more touching than the earnestness and completeness with which Lincoln embraced this idea, and that his "whole soul was occupied" by it.[26]

But the reaction of the nation was not encouraging. Extremists in both camps cried that Lincoln intended to sell them out. The border states remained apathetic, and Congress gave the scheme no more than lip service. The idea languished for a time, then drifted into oblivion. A way to finish the war quickly with justice and fairness to everyone had been condemned to death by a jury of small, selfish and short-sighted men who could not comprehend greatness.

Lincoln's plan, if accepted, might or might not have ended the war as swiftly as he hoped. It certainly would have shortened it by many a month.

9

Resignation

LINCOLN'S STRUGGLE to achieve a quick peace by uprooting slavery had been sincere, persevering, almost frantic. It had been his supreme effort, and had failed. Searing his very soul was the realization that he could not stay the whirlwind he had sown. Disappointment gave way to a wretchedness that was reflected in the melancholy expression of his eyes and the pitiful corrosion of his granite-like features.

The opposition which he had encountered in Congress made him issue his Emancipation Proclamation, but he had not put his name to it without serious misgivings.[1] He had risked disaffection in the army and ridicule from all those who misunderstood his motive. Moreover, the edict lacked one important element of his plan—to effect emancipation through a gradual process. It further broke with an American tradition dating back to the Revolutionary War, when the British had declared all Virginia slaves free. The decree then had been denounced by the American government, and when England repeated the offense in 1812, the Secretary of State again vigorously denied the right of a belligerent to interfere with slavery in enemy territory. Without allowing even the members of his Cabinet a voice in his decision, Lincoln had taken a step which nullified an established American doctrine, and which, in the opinion of a friendly biographer, was "the most momentous . . . since thirteen British colonies had become a nation." The step, he added, also "stood out in startling relief upon the background of popular government and the great free republican system of the world."[2]

Had anyone told Lincoln that posterity would hail him as "The Great Emancipator," he would have shaken his head, smiled his slow, sad smile, and moved his hands deprecatingly. He had signed the Proclamation without enthusiasm. If the border states had behaved sensibly and patriotically, it never would have come into existence. "When in March and May and July, 1862," he would write later, "I made earnest . . . appeals to the border States to favor compensated emancipation, I believed the . . . necessity for military emancipation . . . would come unless averted by that measure. They declined. . . ."[3]

The fighting went on, and Lincoln read the lengthening casualty lists with consternation. He must have remembered with a sinking heart what, fifteen years before, he had said on the floor of Congress about President Polk: ". . . He feels the blood of this war, like the blood of Abel, is crying to Heaven against him . . . originally having some strong motive—which I will

not . . . give my opinion concerning—to involve the
countries in a war, . . . he plunged into it, and has
swept on and on till disappointed in his calculation . . .
he now finds himself he knows not where. . . ."[4]

Lincoln should not have felt the same sense of guilt
which he had ascribed to President Polk. True, both
men had been disappointed in their calculations, but
both had acted in good faith and in the firm belief
that their decisions were in the best interest of the
country. Neither had foreseen the magnitude of the
war he had started but, unlike Lincoln, Polk had made
no effort to avoid it, and had not accepted it as a last
resort, as Lincoln had done.

Lincoln's state of mind began to show in his official
actions. Ever since the beginning of the conflict he
had intervened for soldiers condemned for falling
asleep on sentry duty or other minor offenses. Now
he also stopped the execution of deserters. In one
case he went so far as to order a ruthless departmental
commander to suspend any and all sentences of death
until further notice.[5] On December 8, 1863, he issued
a "Proclamation of Amnesty and Reconstruction," in
which he granted full pardon—with a few exceptions—
to all participants "in the existing rebellion," and full
restoration of their property rights, provided they took
the oath of allegiance.[6] In the next month he extended
this privilege, in a restricted form, to the war prisoners
at Point Lookout, Maryland;[7] and a few weeks later
he directed that all deserters under death sentence be
imprisoned for the remainder of the war or be restored
to duty.[8] To his dismay, however, this attempt to
dampen the war spirit and thereby hasten the advent

of peace failed as completely as had all his previous efforts.

The twin victories of Vicksburg and Gettysburg gave the President momentary relief from his anxieties. Isaac N. Arnold, whom Lincoln once had called the only friend he had in Congress, observed that his "form, bowed and almost broken with anxiety, once more was erect; his eye . . . visibly brighter, and his whole aspect . . . again hopeful."[9] But the joy was short-lived and turned to near despair when Meade let Lee escape across the Potomac. Nevertheless, the Confederacy had suffered a severe setback, and Lincoln wrote hopefully to James C. Conkling in August 1863, "Peace does not appear so distant as it did. I hope it will come soon. . . ."[10]

The appointment of Grant as lieutenant general and prospects for an early victory put new life into the President. His letters began to breathe some of his former spirit. To General Meade, who had asked for a Court of Inquiry, he replied briskly, "I am not impressed, nor do I think the country is impressed, with the belief that your honor demands, or the public interest demands, such an Inquiry. . . . It is much better for you [to] be engaged in trying to do more, than to be diverted. . . ."[11]

But whenever the subject of compensated and gradual emancipation came up, his old wound broke open again. In a letter to A. G. Hodges of Kentucky he expressed renewed regret that the border states had rejected his plan. Then he gave way to his heartache: "Now, at the end of three years struggle the nation's condition is not what . . . any man [had] devised, or expected."[12]

When the Wilderness campaign was about to be launched, the prospects of a new holocaust weighed heavily on the President's conscience. ". . . I am very anxious that any great disaster or the capture of our men . . . shall be avoided," he wrote to Grant.[13] Then his thoughts reverted to the past and some lost opportunities which might have alleviated the country's miseries. He reminded Congress that in 1861 he had recommended the construction of a railroad from Cincinnati to Knoxville, but his advice had been disregarded. As a consequence, the condition of the "most loyal and suffering" East Tennesseans had become lamentable.[14]

He talked poignantly to members of a Maryland delegation whose state had finally adopted emancipation. After congratulating the visitors, he hinted that they should have acted two years sooner. During that time, he told them, the cost of the war had been more than sufficient to bring about the liberation of all the slaves in the country.[15]

Once, in a confidential chat with L. E. Chittenden of the Treasury Department, Lincoln revealed the pangs which plagued him. "We shall have enough to answer for," he sighed, "if we survive this war."[16] It pained him to note that, aside from the common people, few seemed to share his anguish. The generals enjoyed the limelight and were not anxious to see the fighting come to an end. He agreed with Welles, who believed that "they are contented to have the War continue. Never before have they been so . . . magnified."[17] The politicians were more interested in speeches and intrigues than in efforts to end the war. In June 1864 the sponsor of a mass meeting in New York invited Lincoln to attend. The President refused, intimating that the hollowness of the current oratory irritated him. He suggested that the meeting had better turn words into "men and guns."[18] A delegation from Ohio, who congratulated him on his renomination, heard the admonition: "What we want, still more than . . . conventions or presidential elections, is success. . . ."[19]

A few days afterward Lincoln spoke at a Sanitary Fair in Philadelphia, and again bared what was uppermost in his thoughts. The war, he said, was one of the most terrible the world had ever known, in magnitude as well as in duration. "It has deranged business . . . destroyed property, and ruined homes. . . . It has carried mourning to almost every home, until it can almost be said that the 'heavens are hung in black.' Yet it continues. . . . When is [it] to end?"[20]

About this time Lincoln made one more attempt to shorten the war by peaceable means. General Butler, then heading the military department of North Carolina and Virginia, had asked permission to trade with the farmers in his district, so as to weaken their allegiance to the Richmond government. Butler's motives rarely were of the Simon-pure type, but Lincoln was ready to reach for any straw to hasten the end. Butler received his permission[21] but, as could have been foreseen, immediately abused it, thereby destroying a possible instrument for corroding the Confederacy from within. Welles saw it as "a little, dirty, speculating intrigue, . . . to send in plows, harrows, and farming utensils . . . in exchange for cotton and products of the country. . . ."[22] Though the idea had been sound, in Butler's hands its application developed into an ugly scandal, under which Lincoln's noble purpose was ignobly buried.

Disillusionments were piling up on Lincoln, and his mood was reflected in a letter he wrote to Mrs. Gurney, then residing in London. In his letter he managed to say a great deal in very few words. "We hoped for a happy termination of this terrible war long before this; but God . . . has ruled otherwise. . . . He intends some great good to follow this mighty convulsion, which no mortal could make, and no mortal could stay."[23] The emphasis, no doubt, was on the first and last sentences.

How severely Lincoln's cares affected him is illustrated by a conversation he had with the widow of a Northern governor who was attending wounded and sick Union soldiers in occupied Southern territories. She pleaded with the President to have hospitals built in the North, because so many loyal soldiers were dying in the fever-ridden Mississippi River towns. Those lives, she felt confident, could have been saved in healthier and more congenial surroundings.

According to her report, she found Lincoln peevish and querulous. He argued that if the soldiers were moved north, they would desert at the first opportunity, as they had done too often in the past. "This war might have been finished," he said petulantly, "if every man had been in his place who was able to be there."

He probably was referring to the Peninsular campaign, when he recalled that out of 170,000 men whom the Government was paying, only 83,000 could be got into action. "The consequences, you know, proved nearly disastrous," he concluded.

The visiting lady stood her ground, but so did Lincoln; the discussion continued for several days. Finally she assured him that the gratefulness of the soldiers would sustain and relieve his misery. Lincoln bowed his head. "I shall never be glad any more," he said disconsolately.[24]

In August 1864 Farragut forced an entrance into Mobile Bay, and in the following month Sherman took Atlanta. Lincoln's joy was unrestrained, and he gave vent to it in a Proclamation of Thanksgiving. Peace had been brought nearer. If he lived and was re-elected, he would do his utmost to repair the damage the war had caused.

Significantly, Lincoln's invocation of the Divinity steadily grew in frequency as the war proceeded. According to General James F. Rusling, the change had taken place just before the battle of Gettysburg. Rusling may have been right in thinking that the President's "early beliefs were unsettled and variable; but . . . our great War . . . sobered and steadied him." The two men met at the bedside of General Sickles, who had lost a leg in the battle, and when Lincoln was asked if he had been worried about a possible defeat, he replied in the negative. After some hesitation he elucidated his remark. "When everybody seemed panic-stricken," he confided to his listeners, "I went

to my room, . . . locked the door, and got down on
my knees before Almighty God, and prayed to Him
mightily for victory . . . I told him this was his war,
and our cause was his cause. . . . And I then . . . made
a solemn vow . . . that if he would stand by our boys
at Gettysburg, I would stand by him. And he *did*,
and I *will*."[25]

Rusling's report may not be quite accurate, but its
gist sounds true. At any rate, the President's public
pronouncements from then on turned more and more
toward religion. Where he had heretofore only occa-
sionally referred to it, and had to be reminded by Secretary Chase to insert a pious phrase into the Proclamation of Emancipation,[26] he now mentioned the
Deity on every occasion. Replying to the address of a
Methodist delegation on May 14, 1864, Lincoln said,
"God bless the Methodist Church. Bless all the
churches; and blessed be God, who in this our great
trial giveth us the churches."[27] This reply contrasted
strangely with one he had given to a group of ministers
in 1862, to whom he had said sternly that if God
wanted to send him a message, he did not see why it
had to come through them.[28] He was more kindly disposed toward a committee of colored men, who had
presented him with a Bible. After thanking them, he
pronounced their gift as the best which God ever had
given to man.[29]

After the President's re-election in 1864 he responded to a group of serenaders from Pennsylvania
by saying: "I am thankful to God for this approval of
the people. But . . . give thanks to the Almighty. . . ."[30]
Gratitude to the people who had voted for him might

have aroused greater acclaim, but Lincoln had long ago risen above the level of a popularity-seeking politician.

A melancholy overtone crept into the ending of a speech he made from a window of the White House. "The election was a necessity," he said. ". . . It has demonstrated that a people's Government can sustain a national election in the midst of a great civil war. . . . But the rebellion continues. . . ."[31]

Despite the length of Lincoln's first inaugural address, it had contained only short references to the Divinity. The second, delivered four years later, showed the change which since had come over him, for it sounded more like a sermon than a political document:

The Almighty has His own purposes. "Woe unto the world because of offences; for it must needs be that offences come; but woe to that man by whom the offence cometh!" If we shall suppose that American Slavery is one of those offences which, in the providence of God, must needs come, but which, having continued through His appointed time, He now wills to remove, and that He gives to both North and South, this terrible war, as the woe due to those by whom the offence came, shall we discern therein any departure from those divine attributes which the believers in a Living God always ascribe to Him?[32]

In some quarters the President's repeated emphasis on religion elicited a queer response. One day in December 1864 two ladies from Tennessee called on him and asked for the release of their husbands, who were being held as war prisoners. One of the women demanded that her husband, being a religious man, be given preferred treatment. Lincoln agreed to release him, but not without an exhortation. "Tell him," he said, ". . . that I . . . am not much of a judge on religion, but that in my opinion, the religion that sets men to rebel . . . is not the sort . . . upon which people can get to heaven."

How greatly Lincoln suffered by his self-reproach was revealed during one of the rare occasions when he lost his temper. When a Chicago delegation headed by Joseph Medill, publisher of the *Chicago Tribune*, called on him, Lincoln gave them to understand that they had to share with him the guilt of having started the war. "Gentlemen," Medill quoted the President, "after Boston, Chicago has been the chief instrument in bringing this war on the country. . . . It is you who are largely responsible for making blood flow as it has. You called for war until we had it. . . ."[33] So far as is known, this spontaneous outburst is the only utterance which might be construed as an indication that Lincoln considered his war declaration a ghastly mistake, and that his decision had been strongly influenced by the radical elements of his own party.

Other worries about his past actions seemed to disturb the President. In his message to Congress on December 6, 1864, he harked back once more to the theme that slavery was at the root of the war. The Constitutional amendment for emancipation had not passed at the last session. Now he again urged its adoption. Yet his views on the right of the people to decide national issues were no longer the same he had held at the time when he had acted solely on his own responsibility. "The proposed amendment," he explained, "will go to the States for their action . . . the voice of the people now for the first time [will be] heard upon the question."[34] It was as near as Lincoln ever came to admitting publicly that in issuing his Emancipation Proclamation he had acted dictatorially.

The leader of the Confederacy, he continued, could not voluntarily accept re-union, but his followers could, and would be welcomed when they did. After their submission all outstanding questions would be settled by means of legislation, conferences, votes and pardons. It was plain that vindictiveness had no place in his program for the future.

In his endeavor to convince the country of his intended leniency, Lincoln took steps which, in earlier days, would have seriously crippled the war effort. Joshua Speed, his longtime friend, told in a letter to Herndon what had happened ten days before the second inauguration:

When I entered his office . . . I observed, . . . dressed in humble attire, two ladies modestly waiting their turn. . . . The hour had arrived to close the door to all further callers. No one was left in the room now except the President, the two ladies and me. With a rather peevish and fretful air he turned to them and said, "Well ladies, what can I do for you?" . . . From what they said he soon learned that one was the wife and the other the mother of two men imprisoned for resisting the draft in western Pennsylvania. "Stop," said he, "don't say any more. Give me your petition." The

old lady responded, "Mr. Lincoln! we've got no petition. . . ." "Oh," said he, "I understand your cases."
He . . . ordered one of the messengers to tell General
Dana to bring him the names of all men in prison for
resisting the draft in western Pennsylvania. The General soon came with the list. He enquired if there was
any difference in the charges or degrees of guilt. The
General replied that he knew of none. "Well, then,"
said he, "these fellows have suffered long enough . . .
I will turn out the whole flock." . . .[35]

The President's spirit of forgiveness extended to
opponents and political offenders as well. He peremp-
torily rejected recommendations by Stanton and Butler
to mete out punishment by saying, "We must not sully
victory with harshness."[36]

In his Second Inaugural the President again spoke
of his distress at the unexpected length of the war.
"Neither party expected for the war, the magnitude,
or the duration, which it has already attained, . . ." he
said. "Each looked for an easier triumph. . . ." Then
he added, "Fondly do we hope—fervently do we pray
—that this mighty scourge . . . may speedily pass
away."[37]

Early in 1865 Lincoln made one last desperate attempt to finish the war. Immediately upon his return
from the abortive Hampton Roads peace conference
he proposed to renew his offer of buying up all slaves,
including those in the Confederacy, for 400 million
dollars, provided the South would stop fighting prior
to April 1. He sweetened the offer by promising a general pardon for political offenses, a return of all seized

property to its rightful owners, and liberality in all matters not specifically mentioned.

This humane move never reached Congress for the joint resolution Lincoln had intended to recommend, because his Cabinet unanimously rejected the plan. Resignedly he filed it away among his bitterest memories.[38]

On April 11, 1865, Lincoln made his last public address, in which he earnestly advocated an early re-establishment of the old order. Indirectly but forcefully, he declared that inasmuch as the war was virtually over, it was immaterial whether or not the seceded states had been out of the Union. All that mattered was a quick restoration of their practical relations with the rest of the states. In his homely but persuasive way he tried to sow the seeds of good will, hoping that it would replace the hatred which had been engendered.[39]

On April 14 Lincoln penned the last letter he was destined to write. It showed his readiness to stand by his promise that there should be no recrimination, no persecution of the erstwhile enemy. He also confessed that he needed help to carry out this program.

"I thank you for the assurance you give me," he told General Van Alen, "that I shall be supported by conservative men like yourself, in the efforts I may make to restore the Union, so as to make it . . . a Union of hearts and hands as well as of States."[40]

After four years in the White House, after vacillating between idealism and despotism, between shrewd maneuvering and tragic blundering, Lincoln emerged

as a true statesman. When still immature, harassed by
innumerable office seekers, surrounded by men of
doubtful loyalty and compelled to make fateful decisions on the spur of the moment, he had chosen what
he believed would be a short and perhaps bloodless
war as the best solution of the national difficulties.
Given more time, he might have found a way to avert
an armed conflict. It was his misfortune that, contrary
to his calculation, the war turned out to be long and
devastating. When his efforts to stop it were unsuc-
cessful, he did all that was left to him—he vowed to
bind up the nation's wounds and restore a genuine
peace.

He had plunged the country into a long and disastrous war, but would try hard to atone for it. His
words to Van Alen, if fulfilled, would have produced
the results he envisioned. The damage he had caused
could not be eradicated, but he, better than anyone,
could have rebuilt the ruins and inaugurated a new era
of good feeling. He had demonstrated his aim for the
future by having Grant hold out his hand to Lee in
friendship and reconciliation; but Lincoln died before
he could accomplish this aim.

It had been Mr. Lincoln's war; unhappily, it was
not going to be his peace. Little men in high places
took over to sow new seeds of hatred, and the world
would forever ponder the thought which remains as
unfinished as was Lincoln's life work—"If he had
lived on . . . if only Lincoln had lived on. . . ."

Notes

Notes

Chapter 1

1 *The Diary of Gideon Welles* (hereafter cited as "Welles, *Diary*") (Boston: Houghton Mifflin Co., 1911), I, xxxii.

2 *Ibid.;* also p. xl.

3 Ephraim D. Adams, *Great Britain and the American Civil War*, quoted in Jay Monaghan, *Diplomat in Carpet Slippers* (Indianapolis: The Bobbs-Merrill Co., 1945), p. 36.

4 Roy P. Basler (ed.), *The Collected Works of Abraham Lincoln* (hereafter cited as "Lincoln, *Works*") (Brunswick, N. J.: Rutgers University Press, 1953), VIII, 332.

5 Charles W. Ramsdell, "The Natural Limits of Slavery Expansion," *Mississippi Valley Historical Review*, XVI, 168, 171; quoted in J. G. Randall, *Lincoln, the Liberal Statesman* (New York: Dodd, Mead & Co., 1947), p. 24.

6 Jefferson Davis, *The Rise and Fall of the Confederate Government* (hereafter cited as "Davis, *Rise and Fall*") (1881), I, 17 n.

7 *Cong. Globe*, p. 1480, quoted in S. D. Carpenter, *Logic of History* (1864; also published as *Cause of the War* and *Scraps from My Scrap Book*), p. 49.

8 *Appleton's American Annual Cyclopedia* (1861), p. 564, quoted in John Shipley Tilley, *Lincoln Takes Command* (Chapel Hill: University of North Carolina Press, 1941), p. xxix.

9 Quoted among others by Henry J. Raymond, *Lincoln: His Life and Times* (1891), I, 138.

10 Welles, *Diary*, I, 10.

11 Quoted among others by Davis, *Rise and Fall*, I, 281, 282.

12 Howard K. Beale (ed.), *The Diary of Edward Bates* (hereafter cited as "Bates, *Diary*") (Annual Report of the American Historical Association, 1930), IV, 178-180.

13 Lincoln, *Works*, IV, 266.

14 *New York Herald*, December 15, 1860, quoted in Kenneth M. Stampp, *And the War Came* (Baton Rouge: Louisiana State University Press, 1950), p. 184.

15 Nicolay and Hay, *Abraham Lincoln: A History* (hereafter cited as "N. & H.") (New York, 1886-1890), III, 415.

Chapter 2

1 Lincoln, *Works*, IV, 237.

2 *Ibid.*, pp. 240-241.

3 *Ibid.*, p. 261.

4 John T. Morse, *Abraham Lincoln* (American Statesmen Series, 1893), I, 169; Herndon and Weik, *Herndon's Lincoln* (Chicago, 1889), III, 462.

5 Lincoln, *Works*, IV, 159.

6 Harlan Hoyt Horner, *Lincoln and Greeley* (Urbana: University of Illinois Press, 1953), p. 201; also Lincoln, *Works*, IV, 160.

7 Lincoln, *Works*, IV, 162.

8 Morse, I, 211.

9 Lincoln, *Works*, IV, 149-150; N. & H., III, 259.

10 Benjamin G. Smith, Esq., *The War with the South* (New York, 1862), p. 157. The author of this book is given as Benjamin G. Smith, but the part of the book dealing with the early events of the war was written by Robert Tomes, a New York physician and writer.

11 J. G. Holland, *The Life of Lincoln* (1865), p. 288.

12 N. & H., III, 393-394; *Official Records of the . . . Rebellion* (hereafter cited as "*O. R.*" for the Army, or as "*O. R. N.*" for the Navy), *O. R. N.*, series 1, IV, 90.

13 *O. R. N.*, series 1, IV, 109-110.

14 N. & H., III, 378, 394.

15 Abner Doubleday, *Reminiscences of Forts Sumter and Moultrie, 1860-1861* (1876), p. 24.

16 N. & H., IV, 62-63.

17 *O. R. N.*, series 1, IV, 247.

18 Samuel Wylie Crawford, *The Genesis of the Civil War* (1887), pp. 248, 249.

19 *Ibid.*, p. 372.

20 *Confidential Correspondence of Gustavus Vasa Fox* (hereafter cited as "Fox, *Correspondence*") (Publications of the Naval History Society, 1918), I, 36.

21 Crawford, pp. 373, 374.

22 *Ibid.*

23 *Ibid.*, p. 378.

24 *Ibid.*, p. 374.

25 N. & H., III, 395.

26 *Ibid.*, p. 433.

27 *Ibid.*

28. *Ibid.*

29 David C. Mearns (ed.), *The Lincoln Papers* (Garden City, N. Y.: Doubleday & Co., 1948), II, 509.

30 Crawford, p. 409.

31 *O. R. N.*, series 1, IV, 107.

32 *Ibid.*, p. 108.

33 Crawford, p. 408; N. & H., III, 436-437.

34 *O. R. N.*, series 1, IV, 90. The order was sent "by command of Lieutenant-General Scott," not by Welles, as Nicolay and Hay erroneously state (IV, 12).

35 Crawford, p. 425. Crawford's professional opinion, as assistant surgeon at Fort Sumter, was that the men could hold out three days without food.

36 *Ibid.*, p. 391.

37 *Ibid.*, p. 393.

38 *Ibid.*, pp. 393, 394.

39 N. & H. (IV, 32) thought Harvey had blundered—one of the indications that at this time they did not enjoy Lincoln's full confidence.

40 Welles, *Diary*, I, 32.

41 Resumés of the Lincoln-Baldwin conference may be found in Charles W. Ramsdell, "Lincoln and Fort Sumter," *The Journal of Southern History*, August 1937; and in David M. Potter, *Lincoln and His Party in the Secession Crisis* (New Haven, Conn.: Yale University Press, 1942), pp. 356-358.

42 *The Lincoln Papers* contain a letter from George Plummer, a West Virginian, to John May, dated January 9, 1863, the contents of which differ from the account given here in one respect—that Lincoln insisted on a resolution by the Convention to adhere to the Union. Lincoln authorized Hay to confirm the substantial correctness of Plummer's recollections. (For this information I am indebted to the late Benjamin P. Thomas.)

43 For earlier offers by Lincoln to vacate Fort Sumter if Virginia would remain in the Union, see Potter, *Lincoln and His Party*, pp. 353-355.

Chapter 3

1 N. & H., 24; *O. R.*, series 1, I, 230; Doubleday, p. 134, asserts that Anderson's request to send off the laborers was granted, and that only a few voluntarily stayed behind. This assertion must be discounted in the light of Crawford's statement to the contrary. Crawford's statement is supported by Nicolay and Hay, who give the number of laborers still present during the bombardment as forty-three. N. & H., IV, 51. See also where N. & H. record (IV, 25) that Lieutenant G. W. Snyder of Anderson's staff, who had been sent to Charleston on an errand, handed Anderson a written report which stated: "The Governor said that orders had been received from Montgomery not to allow any man in the ranks or any laborer to leave . . . ."

2 Robert V. Bruce, *Lincoln and the Tools of War* (Indianapolis: The Bobbs-Merrill Co., 1956), p. 15.

3 A reduction in rations, according to military practice, meant cutting them in two. Anderson followed this practice when he put the reduction into effect.

4 *O. R.*, series 1, I, 211.

5 N. & H., III, 389.

6 Crawford, p. 392.

7 *O. R.*, series 1, I, 285.

8 Doubleday, p. 138. John S. Tilley intimates that Beauregard had not received an order, but only a suggestion to cut the food supply at once. *Lincoln Takes Command*, p. 202. The *Official Records* do not seem to bear out this interpretation.

9 Fox, *Correspondence*, I, 23, 24, 25, 26.

10 *O. R. N.*, series 1, IV, 247-248.

11 Fox, *Correspondence*, I, 20.

12 *Ibid.*, p. 19.

13 Lincoln, *Works*, IV, 424-425.

14 Fox, *Correspondence*, I, 23, 24, 25, 26.

15 *Ibid.*, p. 24; *O. R. N.*, series 1, IV, 235.

16 Crawford, p. 382; *O. R.*, series 1, I, 235.

17 Crawford, p. 398.

18 *Ibid.*, p. 382.

19 *Ibid.*, p. 392.

20 N. & H., IV, 28.

21 *O. R.*, series 1, I, 251-252.

22 N. & H., IV, 28. J. G. Randall states erroneously that the letter was not mailed until the sixth. *Lincoln the President: Springfield to Gettysburg* (New York: Dodd, Mead & Co., 1945), I, 335. Actually the letter was mailed immediately after having been copied in the War Department, and was received by Anderson in the afternoon of the seventh. Crawford, p. 382. The regular mail between Washington and Charleston required three days for delivery, which confirms that the letter was mailed on the fourth. It should have reached Anderson in the forenoon of the seventh, but probably was delayed while it was being read and copied by the Confederate authorities.

23 Crawford, p. 384.

24 N. & H., IV, 30.

25 Mary Boykin Chesnut, *A Diary from Dixie* (New York: Appleton-Century-Crofts, Inc., 1905), p. 32.

26 Crawford, p. 396 (facsimile of message).

27 Fox, *Correspondence*, I, 39.

28 *O. R. N.*, series 1, IV, 248.

29 Fox, *Correspondence*, I, 23, 24, 25, 26.

30 *Ibid.*, p. 33.

31 *Ibid.*, pp. 23, 24, 26.

32 *O. R. N.*, series 1, IV, 109.

33 Crawford, p. 412.

34 *Ibid.*

35 Fox, *Correspondence*, I, 28.

36 *Ibid.*, p. 29.

37 *Ibid.*, p. 2.

38 Welles, *Diary*, I, 29, 30; N. & H., IV, 7.

39 N. & H., IV, 9.

40 *Ibid.*, p. 36.

41 Crawford, p. 418.

42 Fox, *Correspondence*, I, 14.

43 *Ibid.*, p. 35.

44 *O. R. N.*, series 1, IV, 252.

45 Crawford, p. 417; *O. R. N.*, series 1, IV, 249.

46 *Ibid.*, series 1, IV, 253.

47 *Ibid.*

48 *Ibid.*, p. 249.

49 *Ibid.*, p. 244 (Fox's report, April 19, 1861).

50 Welles, *Diary*, I, 22.

51 *O. R. N.*, series 1, IV, 251; Crawford, p. 418.

52 Fox, *Correspondence*, I, 32.

53 *O. R. N.*, series 1, IV, 249-250.

54 *Ibid.*, p. 245.

55 Fox, *Correspondence*, I, 33, 35.

56 *Ibid.*, p. 27.

57 Welles, *Diary*, I, 23-24; N. & H., IV, 5-6.

58 Morse, I, 249-250.

59 Fox, *Correspondence*, I, 41.

60 *Ibid.*, p. 2.

61 Theodore C. Pease and J. G. Randall (eds.), *The Diary of Orville Hickman Browning* (hereafter cited as "Browning, *Diary*") (Springfield, Ill., 1925), I, 476.

62 Crawford, pp. 398, 399.

63 *Ibid.*, p. 392.

64 Fox, *Correspondence*, I, 36.

65 Lincoln, *Works*, IV, 350.

66 Davis, *Rise and Fall*, I, 289.

67 Fox, *Correspondence*, I, 35.

ACCORDING TO Mrs. Fox, who kept a diary, Lincoln invited her husband to a Cabinet meeting on or about April 5 and promised him the position of Assistant Secretary of the Navy at $3500 a year, if Congress would consent to create this office. Mrs. Fox also was told that "Gus helped make out the War and Navy orders" pertaining to the action which the expedition was to take at Charleston. Inasmuch as Fox violated these orders later, this item is interesting. So is her entry on April 11 that "the paper stated the President considered the expedition merely an experiment; he considered it necessary to send it without regard to its success." Mrs. Fox gives no indication which paper she had read.

On April 17 Mrs. Fox recorded an incident which Fox himself did not mention in his *Confidential Correspondence*. "The *Powhatan*," she wrote, ". . . [was] sent off *two days before he left* to some other destination and without *informing* him, though he had impressed on them to let him know if they made any alteration in the arrangements." It is unfortunate that Mrs. Fox does not identify "them," to whom Fox made this reasonable and precautionary request, nor what assurance, if any, he had been given.

While Mrs. Fox's statements are not without value, it must be remembered that they were based largely on hearsay evidence, and therefore should be evaluated accordingly.

A copy of Mrs. Fox's diary is in the possession of Mr. Robert Bruce, author of *Lincoln and the Tools of War* (The Bobbs-Merrill Company, Inc., 1956) and I am greatly indebted to his generosity.

Chapter 4

1 N. & H., III, 109.
2 "The Diary of a Public Man," *The North American Review*, August-November 1879 (reprint by Abraham Lincoln Book Shop, Chicago, 1945), p. 37.
3 N. & H., III, 442.
4 *Ibid.*, IV, 78.
5 *Ibid.*, III, 441.
6 James G. Blaine, *Twenty Years in Congress* (1884), I, 290.
7 Lincoln, *Works*, IV, 269.
8 *Ibid.*, p. 253.
9 Morse, I, 77.
10 L. E. Chittenden, *Recollections of President Lincoln and His Administration* (1891), p. 75.
11 *Ibid.*
12 James F. Rhodes, *History of the United States from Compromise of 1850* (hereafter cited as "Rhodes") (1892-1895), III, 254, 255.
13 Horace Greeley, *Recollections of a Busy Life* (1868), p. 397.
14 Crawford, p. 312.
15 N. & H., IV, 71.
16 Herndon and Weik, *Herndon's Lincoln: The True Story of a Great Life* (1889), II, 282.
17 N. & H., III, 395.
18 Crawford, p. 366.
19 At that time the *Chronicle* was the only Washington paper which issued a Sunday edition.
20 Lincoln, *Works*, IV, 332.
21 Morse, I, 231.

22 Bates, *Diary*, p. 271.

23 Mrs. Jefferson Davis, *Jefferson Davis, A Memoir* (1890), p. 80.

24 Welles, *Diary*, I, 12.

25 N. & H., IV, 261.

26 *Ibid.*

27 *Ibid.*, p. 228.

28 Rhodes, III, 398.

29 Crawford, p. 447.

30 Randall, *Lincoln the President*, I, 351.

31 Isaac Arnold, *Life of Lincoln* (1884), p. 248.

32 Welles, *Diary*, I, 13.

33 Edward A. Pollard, *The Lost Cause* (1866), p. 108.

34 Davis, *Rise and Fall*, I, 292.

35 B. G. Smith, *The War with the South*, I, 158.

36 John G. Nicolay, *The Outbreak of the Rebellion* (1881), p. 55.

37 N. & H., IV, 44-45.

38 Welles, *Diary*, I, 40.

39 Potter, *Lincoln and His Party*, Chapter IX.

40 *Ibid.*, p. 229.

41 George W. Julian, *Political Recollections* (1883), p. 190.

42 Doubleday, p. 125.

43 Lincoln, *Works*, V, 241.

44 N. & H., III, 333.

45 Lincoln, *Works*, IV, 424 (Message to Congress, July 4, 1861).

46 N. & H., III, 419.

47 Donn Piatt in Allen T. Rice (ed.), *Reminiscences of Abraham Lincoln by Distinguished Men of His Time* (New York, 1886), p. 477.

48 N. & H., IV, 85.

49 Chittenden, *Recollections of President Lincoln*, 76.

50 *The Reminiscences of Carl Schurz* (Garden City, N. Y.: Doubleday, Page & Co., 1917), II, 229, 230.

51 Fox, *Correspondence,* I, 5.

52 Browning, *Diary,* p. 453.

53 Arnold, *Life of Lincoln,* p. 193.

54 Potter, *Lincoln and his Party,* pp. 309, 310.

55 *Ibid.,* pp. 312, 313.

56 Pollard, *The Lost Cause,* 27.

Chapter 5

1 *Dictionary of American Biography* (New York: Charles Scribner's Sons, 1946).

2 *Ibid.*

3 *Ibid.*

4 Browning, *Diary,* pp. 480, 481.

5 N. & H., IV, 32 n.

6 Welles, *Diary,* II, 248.

7 *O. R. N.,* series 1, IV, 245 ff.

8 *Ibid.,* p. 248.

9 *Ibid.*

10 Fox, *Correspondence,* I, 43.

11 *Ibid.,* p. 14.

12 *Ibid.,* p. 7.

13 *Ibid.,* p. 44.

14 Browning, *Diary,* p. 476.

15 Ramsdell, "Lincoln and Fort Sumter," p. 288.

16 Fox, *Correspondence,* I, 36.

17 *Ibid.,* pp. 34, 35.

Chapter 6

1 Raymond, *Lincoln,* I, 175.

2 N. & H., IV, 140.

3 *Ibid.,* pp. 164, 165.

4 N. & H., III, 143.

5 *Ibid.*, pp. 237, 238; Potter, *Lincoln and His Party*, pp. 274, 276.

6 Quoted among others by J. G. Randall, *Constitutional Problems Under Lincoln* (Urbana: University of Illinois Press, 1951), p. 121.

7 N. & H., VIII, 28.

8 Lincoln, *Works*, V, 242.

9 Randall, *Constitutional Problems*, pp. 52 ff.

10 Raymond, *Lincoln*, I, 181.

11 Chittenden, *Recollections of President Lincoln*, pp. 345 ff.

12 William H. Russell, *My Diary North and South* (hereafter cited as "Russell, *Diary*") (1863), p. 535.

13 Chittenden, *Recollections of President Lincoln*, p. 34; Morse, I, 190.

14 *New York Tribune*, August 25, 1862, quoted in Horner, *Lincoln and Greeley*, p. 273.

15 *The Reminiscences of Carl Schurz*, pp. 285, 286.

16 Rhodes, III, 514.

17 Welles, *Diary*, I, 549.

18 *Ibid.*, II, 206.

19 Quoted among others in Davis, *Rise and Fall*, II, 8.

20 Randall, *Constitutional Problems*, p. 31.

21 Bates, *Diary*, p. 331.

22 Blaine, *Twenty Years in Congress*, I, 373.

23 Carpenter, *Cause of the War*, p. 88.

24 *Ibid.*, p. 200.

25 *Ibid.*, pp. 200, 201.

26 *Ibid.*, pp. 201, 316

27 *Ibid.*, p. 202.

28 *Ibid.*

29 *Ibid.*, p. 206.

30 *Ibid.*, p. 202.

31 *Ibid.*, p. 203.

32 *Ibid.*

33 *Ibid.*, p. 213.

34 Quoted in Randall, *Constitutional Problems,* p. 31.

35 N. & H., III, 248.

36 Carl Sandburg, *Abraham Lincoln: The War Years* (New York: Harcourt, Brace & Co., 1939), I, 213.

Chapter 7

1 Crawford, p. 129.

2 N. & H., IV, 375.

3 Sandburg, *Abraham Lincoln,* I, 299.

4 Raymond, *Lincoln,* I, 202.

5 N. & H., IV, 360.

Chapter 8

1 Lincoln, *Works,* V, 48.

2 *Ibid.*

3 *Ibid.,* 49.

4 *Ibid.,* 48-49.

5 N. & H., V, 208.

6 Lincoln, *Works,* V, 145.

7 *Ibid.,* 144-145. Gradual emancipation in the border states had been suggested in a resolution offered in the New York Assembly on February 11, 1862, by Representative McKean, but failed to pass. Rhodes, III, 269, 270.

8 Lincoln, *Works* (Federal edition, 1906), V, 446 ff.

9 Morse, II, 23; Arnold, *Life of Lincoln,* p. 249.

10 Lincoln, *Works,* V, 158.

11 Morse, I, 138.

12 *Ibid.,* pp. 132, 133.

13 N. & H., V, 216.

14 Lincoln, *Works,* V, 223.

15 *Ibid.,* p. 478.

16 *Ibid.,* pp. 317-319.

17 N. & H., VI, 342.

18 Randall, *Constitutional Problems,* p. 255.

19 Lincoln, *Works,* V, 436.

20 Welles, *Diary,* I, 150.

21 *Ibid.,* p. 70.

22 N. & H., VI, 434; Randall, *Constitutional Problems,* pp. 377, 378.

23 Welles, *Diary,* I, 145.

24 Lincoln, *Works,* V, 388.

25 *Ibid.,* p. 518 (Message to Congress, December 1, 1862).

26 Randall, *Lincoln the President,* II, 145.

Chapter 9

1 N. & H., VI, 434.

2 Morse, II, 115.

3 N. & H., VI, 431 (letter to A. G. Hodges, April 4, 1864).

4 Herndon and Weik, *Herndon's Lincoln,* II, 278.

5 Lincoln, *Works,* VII, 59 (telegram from Lincoln to Butler, December 10, 1863): "Please suspend execution in any and all sentences of death in your Department until further orders."

6 *Ibid.,* p. 53.

7 *Ibid.,* p. 103.

8 *Ibid.,* p. 208.

9 Arnold, *Life of Lincoln,* p. 327.

10 N. & H., VII, 384.

11 Lincoln, *Works,* VII, 273.

12 *Ibid.,* p. 282.

13 *Ibid.,* p. 324.

14 *Ibid.,* p. 321.

15 Noah Brooks, *Washington in Lincoln's Time* (1896), p. 203.

16 Chittenden, *Recollections of President Lincoln,* p. 329.

17 Welles, *Diary,* I, 368.

18 Lincoln, *Works*, VII, 374.

19 *Ibid.*, p. 384.

20 *Ibid.*, p. 394.

21 Welles, *Diary*, II, 56; for details see Robert S. Holzman, *Stormy Ben Butler* (New York: The Macmillan Co., 1954), pp. 144, 146.

22 *Ibid.*

23 Lincoln, *Works*, VII, 535.

24 Holland, *The Life of Lincoln*, pp. 443-450.

25 William Hayes Ward, *Lincoln, Tributes from His Associates* (1895), pp. 22, 23.

26 N. & H., VI, 415, 418.

27 Raymond, *Lincoln*, II, 618.

28 McPherson's *History of the Rebellion*, p. 231, quoted in Arnold, p. 259.

29 Lincoln, *Works*, VII, 542.

30 *Ibid.*, VIII, 96.

31 N. & H., IX, 380.

32 Lincoln, *Works*, VIII, 333.

33 Ida M. Tarbell, *The Life of Abraham Lincoln* (New York: Doubleday & McClure, 1900), II, 149.

34 Lincoln, *Works*, VIII, 149.

35 Herndon and Weik, *Herndon's Lincoln*, III, 525.

36 N. & H., IX, 382.

37 Lincoln, *Works*, VIII, 332-333.

38 N. & H., X, 133-135.

39 Lincoln, *Works*, VIII, 399.

40 *Ibid.*, 413.

Bibliography
and
Index

Bibliography

Arnold, Isaac. *The Life of Abraham Lincoln.* Chicago, 1884.

Bates, Edward. *The Diary of Edward Bates.* Howard K. Beale, ed. *Annual Report of the American Historical Association,* 1930, IV.

Blaine, James G. *Twenty Years in Congress.* 1884.

Brooks, Noah. *Washington in Lincoln's Time.* New York, 1896.

Browning, Orville Hickman. *The Diary of Orville Hickman Browning.* Theodore C. Pease and J. G. Randall, eds. Springfield, Illinois, 1925.

Bruce, Robert V. *Lincoln and the Tools of War.* Indianapolis: The Bobbs-Merrill Co., 1956.

Carpenter, Samuel D. *Logic of History* (also published as *Cause of the War; Scraps from My Scrapbook*). 1864.

Chesnut, Mary Boykin. *A Diary from Dixie.* New York: Appleton-Century-Crofts, 1905.

Chittenden, L. E. *Recollections of President Lincoln and His Administration.* New York: Harper Bros., 1891.

Crawford, Samuel Wylie. *The Genesis of the Civil War.* New York, 1887.

Davis, Jefferson. *The Rise and Fall of the Confederate Government.* New York: D. Appleton and Co., 1881.

Davis, Varina Howell. *Jefferson Davis, A Memoir.* 1890.

"The Diary of a Public Man." *The North American Review,* August-November, 1879. Reprinted by the Abraham Lincoln Bookshop, Chicago, 1945.

Dictionary of American Biography. New York: Charles Scribner's Sons, 1946.

Doubleday, Abner. *Reminiscences of Forts Sumter and Moultrie, 1861-1865.* New York: Harper and Bros., 1876.

Fox, Gustavus Vasa. *Confidential Correspondence of Gustavus V. Fox.* Robert Means Thompson and Richard Wainwright, eds. New York, 1918-1919.

Greeley, Horace. *Recollections of a Busy Life.* 1868.

Herndon, William H., and Weik, Jesse W. *Herndon's Lincoln.* Chicago, 1889.

Holland, J. G. *The Life of Lincoln.* 1865.

Holzman, Robert S. *Stormy Ben Butler.* New York: The Macmillan Co., 1954.

Horner, Harlan Hoyt. *Lincoln and Greeley.* Urbana: University of Illinois Press, 1953.

Julian, George W. *Political Recollections.* 1883.

Lincoln, Abraham. *Collected Works.* Federal Edition, 1906.

Lincoln, Abraham. *The Collected Works of Abraham Lincoln.* Roy P. Basler, ed. Brunswick, N. J.: Rutgers University Press, 1953.

Mearns, David C. *The Lincoln Papers.* Garden City, N. Y.: Doubleday & Co., 1948.

Monaghan, Jay. *Diplomat in Carpet Slippers.* Indianapolis: The Bobbs-Merrill Co., 1945.

Morse, John T. *Abraham Lincoln.* American Statesmen Series, 1893.

Nicolay, John G. *The Outbreak of the Rebellion.* New York: Charles Scribner's Sons, 1881.

Nicolay, John G., and Hay, John. *Abraham Lincoln: A History.* New York, 1890.

Official Records of the Union and Confederate Armies in the War of the Rebellion (cited as *O. R.*). Washington, D. C., 1880-1901.

Official Records of the Union and Confederate Navies in the War of the Rebellion (cited as *O. R. N.*). Washington, D. C., 1894-1927.

Pollard, Edward A. *The Lost Cause.* Richmond, 1866.

Potter, David M. *Lincoln and His Party in the Secession Crisis.* New Haven, Conn.: Yale University Press, 1942.

Ramsdell, Charles W. "Lincoln and Fort Sumter." *The Journal of Southern History,* August 1937.

Randall, James G. *Constitutional Problems Under Lincoln.* Urbana: University of Illinois Press, 1951.

Randall, James G. *Lincoln, the Liberal Statesman.* New York: Dodd, Mead & Co., 1947.

Randall, James G. *Lincoln the President: Springfield to Gettysburg.* New York: Dodd, Mead & Co., 1945.

Raymond, H. J. *Lincoln: His Life and Times.* 1891.

Rhodes, James F. *History of the United States from the Compromise of 1850.* 1892-1895.

Rice, Allen T., ed. *Reminiscences of Abraham Lincoln by Distinguished Men of His Time.* New York, 1886.

Russell, William H. *My Diary North and South.* Boston, 1863.

Sandburg, Carl. *Abraham Lincoln: The War Years.* New York: Harcourt, Brace & Co., 1939.

Schurz, Carl. *The Reminiscences of Carl Schurz.* Garden City, N. Y.: Doubleday, Page & Co., 1917.

Smith, Benjamin G. *The War with the South.* 1862.

Stampp, Kenneth M. *And the War Came.* Baton Rouge: Louisiana State Press, 1950.

Tarbell, Ida M. *The Life of Abraham Lincoln.* New York: Doubleday McClure Co., 1900.

Tilley, John Shipley. *Lincoln Takes Command.* Chapel Hill: University of North Carolina Press, 1941.

Ward, William Hayes. *Lincoln, Tributes from His Associates.* 1895.

Welles, Gideon. *The Diary of Gideon Welles.* Boston: Houghton Mifflin Co., 1911.

Index

205